Solution-Focused Groupwork

Brief Therapies Series

Series Editor: Stephen Palmer
Associate Editor: Gladeana McMahon

Focusing on brief and time-limited therapies, this series of books is aimed at students, beginning and experienced counsellors, therapists and other members of the helping professions who need to know more about working with the specific skills, theories and practices involving in this demanding but vital area of their work.

Books in the series include:

Solution-Focused Therapy
Bill O'Connell

A Psychodynamic Approach to Brief
Counselling and Psychotherapy
Gertrud Mander

Brief Cognitive Behaviour Therapy
Berni Curwen, Stephen Palmer and Peter Ruddell

Transactional Analysis Approaches to Brief Therapy
Keith Tudor

Brief NLP Therapy
Ian McDermott and Wendy Jago

Solution-Focused Groupwork

John Sharry

SAGE Publications
London ● Thousand Oaks ● New Delhi

ISBN 0-7619-6779-6 (hbk)
ISBN 0-7619-6780-X (pbk)
© John Sharry 2001
First published 2001
Reprinted 2003, 2004 (twice)

SAGE Publications Ltd
1 Oliver's Yard
55 City Road
London EC1Y 1SP

SAGE Publications Inc
2455 Teller Road
Thousand Oaks
California 91320

SAGE Publications India Pvt Ltd
B-42 Panchsheel Enclave
PO Box 4109
New Delhi 110 017

British Library Cataloguing in Publication Data
A catalogue record for this book is available from the British Library

Library of Congress Control Number: 2001132872

Typeset by Mayhew Typesetting, Rhayder, Powys
Printed and bound in Great Britain by
Biddles Limited, King's Lynn, Norfolk

To my parents
For gentle wisdom and devotion

Foreword

This book secures John Sharry's place as one of Ireland's leading brief therapists. It also places him at the forefront of solution-focused groupwork. It is a book that *must* be read by anyone interested in frontline developments in solution-focused therapy and by anyone interested in resource-based groupwork. So thank heavens it's well written! And it is. Sharry has a fluency with language that allows complexity to sit side by side with clarity and ideas to flow across the page – it is a good read. And there is more!

One of the earliest criticisms of books on solution-focused brief therapy and one levelled particularly at its founders, Steve de Shazer and Insoo Kim Berg, was that they were like cook books and 'you can't learn how to do therapy from a cook book'. As my Brief Therapy Practice colleagues and I taught ourselves from Steve de Shazer's 'cook books', *Keys to Solution in Brief Therapy* (1985) and *Clues: Investigating Solutions in Brief Therapy* (1988), we want to applaud John Sharry for adding so creatively to the 'culinary' bookshelf. *Solution-Focused Groupwork* is a book with recipes that describe a step-by-step way to create a solution-focused group. Read the book and run the group. It might not be the best bit of groupwork you'll ever do but if you follow the guidelines it is likely to be close enough!

So what are the ingredients that go into this book? Years of experience: Sharry, through his Parenting Groups Programme has a long track-record of running groups and explaining how they work so others can run them too. *Solution-Focused Groupwork* is in part a product of this experience but it has also been greatly broadened by Sharry's intellectual curiosity. His inspiration and theoretical underpinnings are drawn from a wide range of writings from which he has drawn common threads that support and complement the overriding interest in resources, competency and strength. As the chapters move between theoretical discussions, practical descriptions and topical tips the reader will enjoy the intellectual stimulation, the sense of 'do-ability' and the already-there answers to some of the more difficult questions. As much a good meal as a good (cook) book.

Look out for Sharry's next book!

Chris Iveson
Brief Therapy Practice, London

Preface

Writing this book represents the convergence of two important paths in my work as a therapist and social worker. The first path started with my attendance at a solution-focused therapy workshop in 1992,[1] which challenged me with startling new ideas. After many years of psychodynamic training centred on the premise that we needed to understand problems and to analyse them before they could be solved, I was confronted with the radical idea that this may not be true: not only is it not necessary always to focus on problems, at times it may be unhelpful and counter-productive to creating solutions. This is the simple but far-reaching idea central to solution-focused therapy, which started me on a search to discover more.

In many ways, incorporating solution-focused ideas into my practice was like 'returning home' for me. They seemed to me to dovetail with the principles of person-centred counselling which constituted my first training in counselling and therapy. They reflected my basic belief in the self-healing potential of people: that within a constructive and supportive therapeutic environment, clients could solve most of their own problems. They also liberated me from being an expert, and gave me ways of collaborating with clients trusting their expertise in their own lives.

The second path, which has led to the writing of this book, has been my discovery of the power of groupwork. Groups bring people together and give them access to the support and creativity of one another, which they do not have in individual therapy. Many times, I have witnessed how a group member is deeply touched and helped by another, in a way that I could not have helped them as a professional therapist. Often I feel my role as a facilitator is simply to bring people together in a group and then to 'get out of the way' and let them help one another. I continue to be struck at how therapeutic groups can become crucibles of great healing and change which far outreaches the power of individual therapy alone.

This book attempts to bring together the power of groupwork and solution-focused therapy, highlighting the synergistic possibilities that occur in their union. Solution-focused principles readily apply to short-term groupwork and indeed their potential is expanded and enhanced in the larger arena of the group. In groups, the potential for clients finding solutions to their life problems is greatly enhanced as they not only have access to their own strengths and resources but also to those of the other group members. The aim of solution-focused groupwork is to create a constructive and supportive group culture and thus harness the power of group dynamics to work in harmony with members as they pursue their individual and collective goals.

The book is written for professionals who use groups to help people and who are interested in discovering ways to make their groups become more positively focused and brief, with the power of group process oriented towards solution building rather than problem solving. The book is practice-based rather than theoretical, concentrating on the practicalities of applying solution-focused principles to groupwork rather than describing in detail the Social Constructionist theory and philosophy that underpins them. For readers interested in exploring such theory there are ample references in the text to pursue for further reading (for example de Shazer, 1994; Gergen & McNamee, 1992; O'Connell, 1998). To make the book accessible and practice-based I have illustrated the ideas using a variety of case examples, sample session dialogues and training exercises. Though most of the examples are drawn from my own experience of running groups with children, families and adults in mental health settings, I firmly believe that solution-focused groupwork has much to contribute to other arenas and settings. As you read the book, I encourage you to adapt the ideas to your own particular setting and context.

In writing this book I am not promoting a 'new model' of groupwork. I have been struck at how the principles of solution-focused groupwork have great resonance with many other positive approaches to working with people in groups (which may already influence your work as a group facilitator). In addition, I have great respect for the tradition of longer-term and problem-focused therapies, particularly the impressive work of Irvin Yalom. However in the current climate, which reflects a growing interest in briefer, strengths-based and resource-focused interventions, I believe that solution-focused groupwork makes a necessary contribution. My hope is that as you read the book you will find some new ideas and suggestions, which you can readily apply, to complement and expand your groupwork practice.

Overview of chapters

For the sake of clarity this book is divided into three parts. Part I describes the background, development and principles of solution-focused groupwork. Chapter 1 describes how the approach has emerged within the tradition of group therapy, in particular considering its effectiveness and the cluster of therapeutic factors that give rise to its power. Chapter 2 lists seven practice-based principles of solution-focused therapy and considers how these can apply to groupwork. This chapter will be of particular interest to readers who are less familiar with solution-focused ideas and who wish to see examples of its principles in action. Chapter 3 conceptualises the dynamics of solution-focused groupwork describing how therapists can practically draw upon these dynamics in helping clients achieve their goals. This is an important chapter that describes how to synergistically expand solution-focused principles in a group setting and thus gets to the heart of solution-focused groupwork.

Part II focuses on the lifecycle of a solution-focused group illustrating how a therapist can plan and facilitate a group from beginning to end. Chapter 4 outlines principles for designing and planning groups, for engaging and motivating clients, for selecting and assessing clients and for preparing them for membership. Chapter 5 outlines the structure of solution-focused groups considering how first, middle, last and review sessions might differ, illustrating these ideas with three sample group plans.

Part III describes specific issues in managing group process. Chapter 6 outlines a model for evaluating groups on a session-by-session basis to ensure therapists gain feedback on client progress which they can integrate into future session planning. Chapter 7 considers solution-focused ways of managing 'difficult' or 'resistant' clients who may challenge the facilitator and appear to knock the group off course. Finally, Chapter 8 describes five creative group exercises which can energise flagging groups and mobilise their resources on creative solution building.

A note on language

To avoid unwieldy uses of he/she or him/her, plurals are used where possible when referring to clients and therapists. In specific case examples an attempt is made to alternate between male and female clients and facilitators. The terms therapist and facilitator are used interchangeably throughout the book, referring to any professional who might be running a group.

Note

1. This workshop was facilitated by Cynthia Maynard and Gill Wyse who trained in solution-focused therapy at the Brief Therapy Practice in London.

Acknowledgements

In writing this book, so many people have helped me along the way and I am delighted to acknowledge them here.

Firstly I would like to thank all the colleagues at the Metanoia Institute and Middlesex University, who have helped me write this book as part of my doctorate, particularly Jenifer Elton Wilson, Derek Portwood, Kate Fromant and Gordon Stobart. I am particularly indebted to my Academic Consultant, Michael Carroll, whose belief and practical support made this project happen. Also thanks to Alison Poyner of Sage, and Stephen Palmer and Gladeana McMahon, editors of the Brief Therapy Series, for helping me shape the original book proposal and for providing helpful comments on the way.

Thanks also to Brendan Madden and Melissa Darmody, my partners at the Brief Therapy Group, who have contributed immeasurably to the ideas in this book and who are true innovators and great teachers in the field of brief therapy.

I am indebted to all my colleagues in the Mater Hospital, who have supported me in undertaking this project, especially all my co-facilitators and particularly Jean Forbes who brought balance, humour and sensitive reflection to our groupwork. I am also grateful to Carol Fitzpatrick, who first introduced me to groupwork and whose vision sparked the development of the Parents Plus Programmes.

Thanks also to Scott Miller, of the Institute for the Study of Therapeutic Change and Chris Iveson, of the Brief Therapy Practice in London, both of whom I regard as my brief therapy mentors. Their writing and workshops have been a personal inspiration to me, and I am particularly grateful for their optimism that this book should be written and their belief that I could do it.

So many of my friends have also helped in the writing of the book. Thanks to Ratnabandu who sourced Buddhist stories for me, to Anne Marie Madden who provided me with examples of groupwork, to Conor Owens who helped me think as a narrative therapist, and to my fellow 'doctoral adventurers' Gary McDarby and Phil de Chazal who appreciated my '1000-word-a-day' successes (and particularly Phil who allowed me to 'pinch' his layout design). Also thanks to

Geraldine White who helped me to 'be artistic' and who brought a special sparkle to my life.

I would like to thank my family, especially my parents, brothers and sisters, and in particular my brother Tom who has inspired me to 'follow my bliss'. I would also like to mention my nephews and nieces who bring a lot of joy to my life. Thanks to Daniel, who though only eight, is my greatest critic and already writing his own book.

Finally, I would like to thank the hundreds of families, adults and children, whom I have had the privilege to work with individually and in groups, whose triumphs against adversity have been a constant inspiration to me. They have taught me the most about good practice and the many case examples in this book tell the story of their great talent and skill at finding solutions in their lives.

PART I
BASICS AND BACKGROUND

1

Groupwork and Solution-Focused Brief Therapy

'I will show you Hell,' the Lord said to the rabbi, whom he took to a large room full of miserable looking people. They all sat around an appetising cauldron of food, but none could eat. The only spoons in the room had long handles, which were long enough to reach the cauldron and scoop up some food, but too long to get the food into one's mouth. As a result, all were frustrated and starving.

'I will now show you Heaven,' the Lord said and took the rabbi to another room. This room was identical, with a large group of people sitting around the same cauldron with the same long spoons. But they looked content, satisfied and definitely well-fed.

'What's the difference?' asked the puzzled rabbi.

'Ahh,' replied the Lord, 'The group in the second room have mastered an important skill. They have learnt how to feed one another.'

The above Hasidic story was used by Irvin Yalom and Katy Weers to open their first group for cancer patients in 1973 (Yalom, 1995). It illustrates how group cultures can differ and the powerful influence of others in people's lives for good and sometimes for bad. The therapeutic group aims to create a group culture that is positively influential, so that members can literally learn 'how to feed' one another. In particular, solution-focused groupwork aims to establish collective and mutually beneficial goals and to harness the group's resources and strengths towards empowering members to make realistic steps towards these goals in the short-term. Before describing the principles of the approach in Chapter 2, this chapter outlines the development of solution-focused groupwork, in particular:

1 Tracing the emergence of solution-focused groupwork from traditional longer-term forms of groupwork, in particular looking at the influence of the self-help movement and a growing cultural preference for strengths-based, shorter forms of treatment.

2 Describing the therapeutic factors, which give groupwork its unique power for change, and how these are activated in a solution-focused approach.

3 Evaluating the research evidence for the effectiveness of groupwork in general and of solution-focused groupwork in particular.

The development of solution-focused groupwork

People have always come together in groups to create and achieve things that they could not possibly have done alone, whether this has been to plan or carry out tasks, to teach or learn, or to dialogue about and resolve disagreements. In ancient Irish history there is reference to the mythological 'fifth province' where the kings of all the other provinces would meet to receive counsel and resolve disputes (Colgan McCarthy & O'Reilly Byrne, 1995). This could be conceived as one of the first mediation groups!

It is not surprising, therefore, that psychotherapists, though initially only working with individuals, began to see the need to work with people in groups in order to harness the power of group dynamics. Joseph Hersey Pratt is attributed with organising the first therapeutic groups in 1905 when he brought together groups of tuberculosis patients to monitor their progress and to educate them about the disease and its management (Gladding, 1991; Tudor, 1999). Initially, Pratt conceived of the group as a cost-effective endeavour, as it saved time to educate patients in groups, but he quickly witnessed how much support and encouragement the patients provided to one another. To Pratt's credit he recognised and promoted this positive group influence and thus was one of the first theorists to utilise the therapeutic power of groupwork (Gladding, 1991).

Though psychoanalysis in the 1920s and 1930s primarily concerned itself with intrapsychic conflict and thus individual work with patients, there were some exceptions, notably Adler who used group counselling in prison and child guidance settings (Gazda, 1989). During this time, a major contribution to the development of groupwork was to come from Moreno who used psychodrama with adults and children and who first coined the terms group psychotherapy and group therapy (Gladding, 1991). The 1940s and 1950s are often seen as the beginning of the modern groupwork period. Bion (1961) working at the Tavistock in London, developed a psychodynamic understanding of group process and Kurt Lewin (1951) developed 'field theory', giving insight into group dynamics and how people relate to one another in a group context. Lewin's work was influential in the development of training or T-Groups and the subsequent encounter group movement.

The 1960s were the heyday of group therapy and groupwork and led the *New York Times* to declare that 1968 was the 'year of the group' (Gladding, 1991). There was a rapid growth in the participation in groupwork both by traditional clients and by the general public who attended personal growth groups and encounter groups. The variety and types of groups available also expanded and it was a period of great theoretical diversity. Many of the major humanistic practitioners applied and developed their ideas to group settings. Perls (1967) and Berne (1966) applied gestalt theory and transactional analysis, respectively, to group therapy. Carl Rogers applied his person-centred approach to groupwork and he was instrumental in the development of the encounter group movement, which became a major social phenomenon in America and the rest of the world (Rogers, 1970). Ordinary people, driven by a desire for personal growth and connection with other people, attended encounter groups in large numbers. The 1970s represented a period of consolidation in the development of groupwork. Though participation continued to grow, there was also widespread criticism and an awareness of the potentially damaging effect of groups (Gladding, 1991). Yalom made a major contribution in 1970 with the publication of *The Theory and Practice of Group Psychotherapy*, which provided a research-based and pan-theoretical account of the therapeutic factors inherent in all forms of groupwork (Yalom, 1970).

Influence of brief therapy
Up until the 1980s therapeutic groupwork was generally characterised by a long-term, open-content, open-ended format. Like its parallel, individual psychotherapy, courses of treatment were thought to take several months or even years to complete. However, many research studies during this period found that, even in planned long-term treatments, therapy does not last for an extended time period. In a study of patients referred to open-ended, long-term groups, Stone and Rutan (1983) found that only 8 per cent attended a group for as long as one year. These findings are paralleled in individual therapy where the majority of studies over recent decades have indicated that on average treatments last between four and eight sessions (Garfield & Bergin, 1994). This can lead us to the tentative conclusion that in everyday practice most psychotherapy and counselling, whatever the orientation, is brief.

While traditional groupwork might have been 'inadvertently' brief in many instances, there has been a growing interest in planned brief therapy since the 1980s (Hoyt, 1995; Yalom, 1995). As O'Connell (1998: 6) put it: 'Brief therapy does not mean "less of the same" but therapy with its own structure and process that differs from long term.' Many writers have attempted to characterise the features of these new brief group interventions (Budman & Gurman, 1988; Klein, 1993; MacKenzie, 1994), which are summarised in Box 1.1.

- Clear, specific goals, which can be achieved in the time available.
- The establishing of good group cohesion as soon as possible.
- A focus on present issues and recent problems.
- Client homogeneity: they have similar problems, goals or life experiences.
- Focus on interpersonal rather than intrapersonal concerns.
- The therapist is active, positive and openly influential.

Box 1.1   *Characteristics of brief groupwork*

The increasing popularity of brief groupwork represents a number of paradigm shifts that have taken place in society. There is increasingly a call for therapy to be cost-effective and accountable and for agencies to address the needs of a population of potential service users rather than a small number of clients who avail themselves of long-term therapy. In addition there is a growing customer preference for shorter forms of intervention (O'Connell, 1998). It is now generally recognised that most clients come to therapy believing that their problems will take only a few sessions to resolve (Koss & Shiang, 1994) and there is some evidence that clients will opt for shorter treatment even when they could pursue extra sessions at no cost to themselves (Hoyt, 1995). The emergence of brief groupwork represents a response to the new context in which therapists and clients find themselves.

Influence of self-help groups
Although the first self-help group, Alcoholics Anonymous (AA), was established in the 1930s, it is in the last twenty years that the self-help group movement has really taken off to become a major contributor to positive mental health. Yalom (1995) suggests that the thriving self-help group movement has replaced the encounter movement as the choice for the average person who is looking for the support and encouragement of peers that is to be found in the interpersonal interaction of groups. It is now possible to attend a self-help group for just about every problem or specific issue facing people, whether it is an alcohol or drug problem, being bereaved or affected by suicide, wishing to overcome shyness or recovering from major mental illness. For nearly every medical condition there is now an associated self-help group from which sufferers or their families can seek support. Self-help groups also bring together people who are

stigmatised or alienated in society whether it is on account of being obese, black, gay, a single parent, or from any other minority. They are also a major source of support to people going through common life transitions such as being a new parent, being recently divorced or undergoing retirement. In recent years huge numbers of people in North America have attended a self-help group. A recent study of graduate students in social work and clinical psychology found that nearly 40 per cent of them had personal experience with a self-help group (Meissen, Mason, & Gleason, 1991). A comprehensive survey of the general population in North America in 1991 revealed that approximately 7 per cent of the adult population had attended a self-help group (Wuthnow, 1994). Given that this figure is equivalent to or greater than the take up of professional therapeutic services it is arguable that self-help groups are as important as professional mental health services in providing support to the general public (Corey, 2000; Yalom, 1995).

There are many parallels and overlaps between the development of brief models of groupwork and the development of self-help groups. Both demonstrate the increasing value placed on clients solving problems from their own strengths as opposed to being dependent on a professional facilitator. Indeed, all therapeutic interpersonal groupwork could be conceived as having a 'self-help' component to it. The primary power of a mature or advanced therapy group is the influence of the members on each other. What counts is how members help one another. As we shall see in later chapters, the aim of the facilitator is to establish the conditions and trust in the group whereby clients can help one another and then to 'get out of the way' to allow them to do it. There are also overlaps between brief group-work and self-help groups and the distinction is often blurred. In a survey of self-help groups in North America it was found that between 70 per cent and 80 per cent have some form of professional involvement, whether this is when they were being established or on a consultancy basis at different periods during their lifetime (Goodman & Jacobs, 1994). Conversely, many brief groups have gone on to become functioning self-help groups or have relied on clients from associated self-help groups to assist in their facilitation. Arguably, every brief group therapist should aim to transform the group they are facilitating into a self-led, self-help group – the ultimate in brief groupwork, having no professional involvement whatsoever!

Influence of solution-focused therapy

Solution-focused therapy has its origins within the family therapy/ systemic tradition and derives mainly from the work of de Shazer, Berg and their colleagues at the Brief Therapy Centre, Milwaukee,

Table 1.1 *Comparison of problem/pathology and solution/strengths approaches*

Problem-focused	Solution-focused
Focuses on understanding fixed problem patterns in clients' lives.	Focuses on understanding how change occurs in clients' lives, and what positive possibilities are open to them.
Elicits detailed descriptions of problems and unwanted pasts.	Elicits detailed descriptions of goals and preferred futures.
Person is categorised by the problems and diagnoses they have.	Person is seen as more than the problem with unique talents and strengths, and a personal story to be told.
Focuses on identifying 'what's wrong', 'what's not working' and on deficits in individuals, families and communities.	Focuses on identifying 'what's right and what's working', on strengths, skills and resources in individuals, families and communities.
Clients invariably resist change or therapy, and may prefer the secondary gains of the problem.	'Resistance' is created when the therapeutic goals or methods, or the therapeutic alliance do not fit with the client. The onus is on the therapist to adapt therapy to the clients' goals, to their preferred method and to create a constructive alliance.
Therapy has to be long-term to create enduring change.	Therapy can be brief in creating 'pivotal' change in clients' lives.
Trauma invariably damages clients and predicts later pathology.	Trauma is not predictive of pathology as it may weaken *or strengthen* the person. The therapist is interested in discovering how the client has coped with the trauma.
Centrepiece of therapy is the treatment plan devised by the therapist who is the 'expert'.	Centrepiece of therapy is the clients' goals, coupled with their strengths, resources and expertise on their own lives, to move towards them.

Source: Parts of this table were adapted from Saleeby (1996)

USA (de Shazer et al., 1986). It differs from many traditional therapies in that its focus is not on the problem, its cause and development, but on the solution, preferred futures, and goals. Table 1.1 compares the assumptions which underpin problem-focused and solution-focused approaches to therapy.

When solution-focused therapy was developed the approach represented a paradigm shift from the largely pathology-centred therapies, which were prominent in psychotherapy. O'Hanlon and Weiner-Davies (1989) described the development as a 'megatrend' in psychotherapy: 'Stated simply, the trend is away from explanations, problems and pathology, and towards solutions, competence and capabilities' (p. 6). This 'megatrend' is mirrored in many other developments in therapeutic methods which emphasise a strengths-based orientation such as narrative therapy (White & Epston, 1990), strengths-based approaches in social work (Saleeby, 1992) and the resilience focus developed in family therapy (Walsh, 1996).

Since the development of the model, solution-focused therapy has been applied to groupwork in a range of settings and with a range of client populations, such as in schools with children and adolescents (LaFontain, Garner, & Boldosser, 1995), relaxation groups in mental health day centres (Schoor, 1995), patients in psychiatric hospital (Vaughn, Hastings-Guerrero, & Kassner, 1996), parenting groups (Selekman, 1993) and perpetrators of domestic violence (Uken & Sebold, 1996). Solution-focused ideas have also been combined with other cognitive-behavioural models in anger management groups (Schoor, 1997) and parent training groups (Sharry, 1999, in press).

The therapeutic factors of solution-focused groupwork

Within solution-focused therapy clients are seen as having most of the resources and strengths to solve their own problems (George, Iveson, & Ratner, 1990). Therapy is ideally a process of empowerment, where clients are 'reconnected' to the resources that exist within their lives and encouraged to take charge of their own healing. Brief groupwork with its emphasis on bringing people together to support and encourage one another towards similar goals also espouses values of empowerment and self-healing, but gives members access not only to their own resources but also to those of other group members. In addition, individuals can bind together in groups and take on outside oppressive forces in society, which give rise to the problems, in ways that would not be possible alone. For example, in groups members of a racial minority are in a better position to raise awareness and challenge any discrimination directed towards them.

In this way, solution-focused therapy is ideally situated within groupwork, as many of its principles resonate with the therapeutic factors inherent in groupwork. Yalom (1970, 1995) was one of the first theorists to analyse comprehensively the therapeutic factors inherent in group therapy which give rise to its unique power as distinct from individual therapy. Solution-focused groupwork can be conceived as aiming to 'activate' the therapeutic factors of groupwork. In a well-functioning solution-focused group the group dynamics have been harnessed in such a way as to work in harmony

Table 1.2   *Therapeutic factors of groupwork*

Solution-focused groupwork	Yalom's (1995) therapeutic factors
Group support	Universality (sense of not being 'only one') Group Cohesiveness Catharsis
Group learning	Imparting of information Interpersonal learning Developing socialising techniques Imitative behaviour Corrective recapitulation of the primary family group
Group optimism	Instillation of hope
Opportunity to help others	Altruism
Group empowerment	*no equivalent*
no equivalent	Existential factors

with the members in the pursuit of their goals. Yalom's original list of therapeutic factors applied to all types of groups. Given the brief and focused nature of solution-focused groupwork, different clusters of factors are prominent. These are listed in Table 1.2. The table includes Yalom's concept of 'existential factors' (facing the basic issues of life, death, freedom, isolation and meaning) though it has no obvious equivalent in solution-focused groupwork and also the factor of 'group empowerment' (whereby groups develop their own identity collectively to take action in the outside world), which has no simple equivalent in Yalom's original list.

Group support
Many clients come for professional help burdened by the idea that they are the 'only ones' with a particular problem. They feel blamed by others and frequently blame themselves. They often feel that their thoughts or feelings are unacceptable or shameful and shared by no one else. Such self-blame is an enormous block to therapeutic progress. The sense of universality that groups can bring is very powerful in alleviating this burden, often in a way that is not possible in individual work alone. For example, clients who have been bereaved can often harbour difficult-to-bear or unacceptable feelings. They can feel a great deal of anger at the lost loved one for having left or, more unacceptable still, they can even feel great relief that the person is dead. Though such feelings are relatively common, clients can experience great guilt at having them and this can block any healing. In groups, clients can draw enormous support

in realising that they are not alone in their experience, no matter how awful it is; it is great solace that other people have felt the same way. In fact one of the most common pieces of written feedback from clients who have completed group interventions is how relieved they felt when they realised they were 'not the only one'.

Group facilitators can use the great power of universality by designing specific issue groups that bring clients together who are coping with similar problems such as sexual abuse survivor groups, carers groups, bereavement groups, etc. Even in groups where there are cultural or other differences among members, the group facilitators can enhance the sense of universality by ensuring a common purpose in the group formation and by focusing on common experiences in facilitating the group.

The sense of being understood and accepted differs in a group context than in individual work, as within a group the client experiences this acceptance from fellow members as well as the facilitator. Clients may find it more powerful and a bigger boost to self-worth to be understood by their peers than by a professional facilitator alone. Equally, in a group there are many more personalities and different types of people. Clients are more likely to find someone 'on their wavelength' in this mixture and there can be a richness and diversity in the types of relationships possible. In many brief groups clients have made friendships and alliances that have endured beyond the life of the group and which have been arguably more helpful than previous professional relationships.

Group learning
Successful individual therapy generally involves a degree of learning on the part of the client, whether this is information supplied by the therapist (for example, many addiction counsellors provide information on the effects of drugs to their clients) or interpersonal learning, whereby the client becomes aware of how they personally relate to the therapist and can generalise this to outside relationships. A group setting can provide a more rich and diverse environment for learning and can have a more powerful impact on the individual.

Groups can afford a more empowering way for information to be imparted. On a one-to-one basis, the imparting of information can appear hierarchical and didactic and can take away from the normally facilitative therapeutic role of the professional. In a group, there is the opportunity for the discussion and debate of presented ideas. Members can feel more empowered to challenge ideas and thus not to take them at face value but to adapt them to their own life situation. Secondly, in a group setting members have the opportunity to learn from each other. Learning can become a shared collaborative endeavour, each person as well as the facilitator imparting information to the group.

The group setting also provides an excellent opportunity for interpersonal learning. Clients can gain insight into their relationships with others, both by relating differently themselves and by observing and learning from how others relate. In solution-focused groups, this is often achieved directly by the use of role-play or structured exercises. For example, when teaching communication skills, role-play could be used to give clients an experience of relating differently, with learning being reinforced by feedback from other group members. Equally, interpersonal learning could occur indirectly. Clients are indirectly learning from each other all the time as they experience and observe the interactions in the group. In a solution-focused group, the facilitator can build on this by focusing on positive patterns of communication in the group, drawing members' attention to them. For example, a facilitator could notice: 'I admire the way Jean spoke up then and clearly said what she thought, while also listening to Gerry.' Such a positive focus can enhance interpersonal learning.

From a solution-focused perspective the goal in groupwork is to create a culture of positive, supportive interpersonal communication among the group members. Many clients come from family or outside group situations that are problematic and stressful. The aim of solution-focused groupwork is not to repeat negative patterns of communication, for understanding or analysis, but to provide a 'positive exception' to them. The group should become an enjoyable learning and therapeutic experience for members.

Group optimism
Hope and optimism are essential preconditions to therapeutic change. Over and over again researchers have proven how expectation or hope of change on the part of the client or the therapist (commonly called placebo factors) can have a very powerful effect on outcome (Snyder, Michael, & Cleavins, 1999). In clinical studies in the treatment of depression researchers have found that an inert placebo can be as powerful as psychoactive drugs, when patient and/ or doctor believe that it is going to work (Greenberg & Fisher, 1997). So important is the instillation of hope, that Lambert (1992) in a widely cited survey of psychotherapy outcome estimated that placebo factors were *as important as* therapeutic technique and skill in creating a positive outcome (both accounting for 15 per cent of the variance in positive outcome).

Groups also afford unique ways to foster hope and the expectation of change, which are not available in individual work. The creation of a group is often perceived as a dramatic event by clients; the fact that several people are coming together united in a common cause can instil more hope than a single person alone. Solution-focused group facilitators can capitalise on this fact by presenting the purpose of the group in a positive light to potential members. By emphasising the goals of the group and the strengths of the individual members a facilitator can build a strong belief in the potential of the group.

Secondly, in groups clients witness other people who are solving or who have solved problems similar to their own and this can give them great hope that such change is also possible in their own lives. Group facilitators can capitalise on this by ensuring that the primary orientation of the group is solution-focused, centred on how members cope with and solve problems and on their strength in overcoming limitations and surviving adversity. It can also be helpful to involve 'successful graduates' of previous groups in the running of subsequent ones. For example, in a college setting it can be very powerful to invite a student who successfully completed a previous group to be a co-facilitator. The other students are often more convinced by the experience of this person who is of a similar age and background to themselves. Hearing the student's positive and real account of change can inspire them to believe that change is also possible in their own lives.

Opportunity to help others
A not-so-obvious therapeutic factor in groupwork is the opportunity it affords group members an opportunity to help others. As Yalom (1995: 12) notes:

> Psychiatric patients beginning therapy are demoralized and possess a deep sense of having nothing of value to offer others. They have long considered themselves as burdens, and the experience of finding that they can be of importance to others is refreshing and boosts self-esteem.

The mutual help provided in groups can be a vast resource and an alternative to the 'expert' help of professionals. Indeed, group members are often much more likely to accept the support, suggestions and encouragement of other group members who are seen as on their level than that of the professional facilitator, who is seen as distinct from them. The act of helping benefits the helper as well as the helped. Rappaport, Reischl and Zimmerman (1992) describe how the roles of group and organisational leadership are enormously beneficial to senior members of the GROW programme (a twelve-step self-help programme for former mental patients). Indeed they note that:

Members who provided more helping behaviors to others in the group meetings (assessed by detailed behavioral observations) showed both higher rates of attendance and greater improvement in social adjustment over time. (1992: 87)

The opportunity to help others in groupwork gives members a chance to be of value and to contribute meaningfully to the group and thus be valued themselves. It also gives members a distraction from self-absorption in their own problems, and thus can give a new perspective. The act of helping necessitates listening to and focusing on the concerns of another; helping makes group members reach outside themselves to consider the position of another. By doing this they gain a different and often more grounded perspective on their own problems.

Group facilitators can enhance this therapeutic factor by collaboratively running groups with clients and by looking to involve them in all aspects of the group functioning, drawing on their strengths, resources and skills. This can be as simple as asking one group member to describe how he/she overcame a bout of depression to another member who is feeling low that day. Equally facilitators can ensure there are many roles of responsibility for members to take up in the design and facilitation of the group. Over time there may be an opportunity to step down from leadership and ultimately empower the group to run itself (perhaps stepping in from time to time as a consultant), thus allowing members to benefit maximally from the dual roles of helping and being helped.

Group empowerment
Therapeutic groups can become powerful forces in their own right and can influence outside arenas within society at large. Group members with common experiences, bound together in a common purpose, can feel empowered to take on outside forces and to address the issues that they may not have been able to do alone. In addition, by being in a group with complementary resources, they can have much greater impact than as single individuals operating alone. Whether this is a group of women who have suffered domestic violence campaigning for better protective legislation and for change in societal attitudes, or whether it is a parents' group in a special school working together to promote an awareness of the needs of parents with disabled children and lobbying for better facilities, in both cases the group members have been empowered to take their cause outside the confines of the group to impact on wider issues.

Narrative therapists believe that many problems are caused by outside forces and should not be exclusively located within the individual (Madigan, 1998; White & Epston, 1990). For example, anorexia could be conceived as being created (or certainly propagated) by societal attitudes towards women in general and the female body in particular. If the problem is to be solved then the individual needs to be empowered to take on and challenge these distorted ideas which permeate society. Empowerment is about externalising the problem outside the individual and locating its cause in oppressive discourses and ideas that support it. Narrative therapists have discovered that groups can provide a powerful arena for this process to take place. By bringing people affected by the same problems together, powerful 'think tanks' can be established where members share ideas and generate new descriptions and knowledge about the problem which they can then take outside the group to challenge existing prejudices reinforcing the problem's influence. Like the self-help movement this knowledge can have far-reaching consequences and can be of great benefit to other people affected by the problem. This is the purpose of the Anti-Anorexia League (Grieves, 1998; Madigan, 1998) and the 'Power to Our Journeys' group established by the Dulwich Centre Community Mental Health Project (Brigitte, Sue, Mem, & Veronika, 1997). The 'Power to Our Journeys' group consists of a group of women, affected by schizophrenia, who have published documents both on their experiences of schizophrenia and how they have managed to overcome its negative effects. The documents communicate their unique experience and are published as a sign of them taking back control of their lives and in support of other people affected by schizophrenia. In addition, the members of the group act as consultants to the mental health project and they invite contact from similar groups worldwide (Brigitte et al., 1997).

Effectiveness

Is groupwork generally effective?
Though therapeutic groupwork is a broad category including diverse models and approaches, there is a general consensus in the research literature that groupwork is an effective intervention. On average clients receive significantly more benefit by attending a therapeutic group than by being part of a minimal treatment control group and this conclusion is duplicated in numerous studies and borne out in meta-analyses (Bednar & Kaul, 1994).

A second question, which is perhaps more burning for practitioners, is whether groupwork is more effective than equivalent individual work. Smith, Glass and Miller (1980) in their famous meta-study of psychotherapy research found that group therapy was as effective as individual therapy. Toseland and Siporin (1986) in another meta-study reviewed thirty-two comparison studies and found group therapy to be more effective than individual therapy in 25 per cent of the studies and for both modalities to be comparable in outcome in the remaining 75 percent. McRoberts, Burlingame and Hoag (1998) in a more recent meta-review of twenty-three outcome studies found no difference in outcome between the group and individual formats.

In summary, we can conclude that generally groupwork is as effective as individual work and in some instances may actually be more effective. This means of course that conclusively groupwork is a more cost-effective intervention, given that many more clients are helped via groupwork for the same amount of therapist input (or indeed with no therapist input in the case of many self-help groups). Of course it would be naïve to suggest that groupwork should replace individual work. For many clients groupwork is not an option, in that they prefer individual work or the group setting would not meet their needs. In addition many group formats depend on individual work. For example it may be necessary to have a screening interview or a number of preparatory or parallel sessions to facilitate the group intervention being taken up. It is more fair to conceive the modalities of treatment as complementary and interdependent on one another. Providing the option of either individual or groupwork or both to clients is perhaps the best way to maximise outcome.

Is solution-focused groupwork effective?
In order to cope with the large numbers of clients referred for long-term group psychotherapy, Malamud and Machover (1965) arranged fifteen-session preparatory groups for up to thirty patients to prepare them for the subsequent group therapy. The researchers were interested in establishing whether the group preparation had a positive effect on group outcome for the subsequent group therapy. Not only was this found to be true, but many of the patients *had made substantial gains in the preparatory groups deeming it unnecessary for them to start the long-term group therapy.* Thus inadvertently the researchers gave an endorsement of brief groupwork.

With the emergence of brief groupwork as a modality in the 1980s and 1990s, researchers have begun to study its effectiveness. In their review of research Rosenberg and Zimet (1995) found strong evidence that time-limited outpatient group therapy was effective for behavioural, cognitive-behavioural and psychodynamic approaches. Though solution-focused groupwork is a relatively new development, there is a growing body of research to suggest its effectiveness. A study of six-session solution-focused parenting groups found parenting skills were significantly improved in treatment compared to a waiting list control group (Zimmerman et al., 1996). Students who completed solution-focused counselling groups were found to have significantly higher levels of self-esteem and more appropriate coping behaviour than students in a waiting list control group. In addition the solution-focused counsellors reported less 'exhaustion' and 'depersonalisation on one year follow up (LaFontain & Garner, 1996; LaFontain, Garner, & Eliason, 1996). In a study of two separate projects using a solution-focused group intervention with 151 perpetrators of domestic violence treatment, only seven clients (4.6 per cent) had re-offended on completion of the programme (Lee et al., 1997). In a recent six-year follow-up recidivism rates for the clients in the study amounted to 17 per cent (Uken, 1999). These results are very impressive when compared to recidivism rates at five-year follow-up for traditional treatments which are as high as 40 per cent (Shepard, 1992).

Summary

Solution-focused groupwork has emerged within recent years as a realistic model for structuring therapeutic interventions. Its emergence reflects a growing consumer and cultural preference for strengths-based and briefer forms of therapy. The approach works by activating the therapeutic power inherent in bringing groups of people together to help one another, giving rise to increased optimism, support and learning. This empowers members individually and collectively to take action. Though solution-focused groupwork is a relatively new development, there is a growing body of research to suggest its effectiveness as a therapeutic intervention. In addition, the approach arguably has a number of positive implications for practice in that it presents a strengths-based collaborative way of working, which makes the best use of the resources to which clients and professionals have access.

2
The Principles of Solution-Focused Groupwork

A woman had a problem with the pharmacist in her village. She found that most of the time he was brusque and unfriendly when he dealt with her. Over time his rudeness bothered her so much that she decided she had to do something. She could not change her pharmacist, as he was the only one in the village, so she decided she should go and confront him about it. When discussing the dilemma with a friend, the friend suggested that she would go and have word with the pharmacist on her behalf, as the woman was too upset to deal with it herself.

The next week when the woman went to the pharmacist, he was very courteous to her in a way she had rarely seen before. Delighted, she went back to her friend to ask what she had said to him.

'Did you confront him? Did you tell him how upset I was when he was rude?' the woman asked.

'No,' replied the friend, 'nothing like that. I simply said to him that you thought he could be a charming person sometimes and that you appreciated it very much when he was courteous and friendly to you.'

The above story, adapted from one told by Ben Furman and Tapani Ahola in their book *Solution Talk* (Furman & Ahola, 1992), illustrates some of the radical principles of solution-focused therapy and how they differ substantially from the traditional problem-focused approach to problem-solving. The friend could have confronted the pharmacist with the problem, saying that the woman found him rude and unfriendly. However, this could have led to defensiveness on his part and perhaps even more rudeness in the future. Instead the friend identified the goal inherent in the problem (that the woman wanted him to be courteous), and picked out and valued an exception (notably that he could be friendly at times). Such a positive approach is arguably more effective and brief in producing an outcome that is acceptable to all parties.

This chapter practically explores seven underlying principles of solution-focused therapy, considering in particular how they can applied in groupwork.

---

1   Focusing on change and possibilities.
2   Creating goals and preferred futures.
3   Building on strengths, skills and resources.
4   Looking for 'what's right' and 'what's working'.
5   Being respectfully curious.
6   Creating co-operation and collaboration.
7   Using humour and creativity.

Box 2.1   *Principles of solution-focused groupwork*

1 Focusing on change and possibilities

Nothing is permanent but change.

Heraclitus

Clients come to groups in particular and counselling in general looking for change in their lives. They perceive a certain problem or a lack in their life, which appears fixed enough to cause them to seek outside help. Whereas problem-focused therapists are interested in understanding fixed patterns in a client's life, particularly those established around the problem, solution-focused therapists are interested in understanding how change occurs in a client's life. The role of the solution-focused therapist is to identify and amplify positive change that is already happening in the client's life. Even small and apparently insignificant positive changes once identified and owned by the client can lead to more dramatic changes in other areas of the client's life causing a 'ripple effect'. Or as Erickson said, 'Therapy is often a matter of tipping the first domino' (Rossi, 1980: 454). Focusing on positive changes already occurring in clients' lives can create new optimism and build up a momentum for further change.

Pre-session change

De Shazer and his colleagues originally conceived of therapy as 'initiating change' (de Shazer, 1988: xv). They worked with the client in the first session to identify a clear therapeutic goal and then create an intervention designed to bring about change. However, a chance discovery whereby a client described *how many positive changes had already occurred prior to the first session* (between booking and attending), led them to change their approach. In a subsequent study of thirty cases they discovered that 66 per cent of clients reported to having observed positive pre-session changes (Weiner-Davies, de Shazer & Gingerich, 1987). Lawson (1994) in a similar study of eighty-two cases, found that forty-nine (59.75 per cent) reported positive pre-session change with regard to the presenting problem.

Identifying and amplifying pre-session change is very empowering for clients since they have achieved this success independently of the therapist and thus they must take the full credit for it. As change has already started, counselling centred on pre-session events is more likely to be brief and the client is less likely to be dependent on the therapist. In groups pre-session change can be capitalised upon by the facilitator ensuring it is highlighted as important. For example the therapist could preface the first group discussion in the first session as follows:

> *Therapist*: Between the time you decided to do the group and coming here today, a lot of positive changes may have already occurred. I'm always impressed at the amount of work people have already done to solve problems before they come to a group like this. So I'd like to hear, as we begin the discussion, about any changes that have happened, or any positive events that have happened that you would like to happen again.

Pre-session change can also be highlighted by the facilitator asking about it and ensuring any examples get discussed when they arise:

> *Therapist*: What changes have happened since you decided to do the group?
> *Client*: To be honest, some things have improved since a few weeks ago.
> *Therapist*: Really, what is different?
> *Client*: Well, I find I'm getting up a bit earlier. I'm not lounging in bed as long. I'm more motivated.
> *Therapist*: Wow, that's pretty good . . . you're getting up earlier, you're feeling more motivated.
> *Client*: I'm just a little more positive.
> *Therapist*: So already things are beginning to change for you. How have you brought these changes about?
> *Client*: I guess the decision to do something, coming to the group has got me going.
> *Therapist*: That's really interesting. Has anyone else found that? That the decision to come to the group has already got people going.
> *Client2*: Yeah I've found that too.
> *Therapist*: Really, how has that worked for you?

Creating the expectation for change

Attending a group, whether it is a counselling group or an evening class, can become a dramatic event in the life of an individual. Participants often go to great trouble to attend and the fact that many other people are doing likewise can add importance to the endeavour and increase expectations about what it can deliver. Solution-focused groupworkers orient these heightened expectations around positive change. The more they get participants to believe change is possible and to be on the lookout for examples of positive change in their lives, the more successful the group can be. As we shall see in Chapter 4, effective groupwork requires extensive preparation on the part of the facilitator and participants, and it is in the pre-groupwork that core expectations are established, including a focus on positive change. For example in a screening interview the following suggestion can be given to a potential participant:

> *Therapist*: Attending the group has been very helpful to many participants in creating the changes they want in their lives. For some people this has been quite dramatic. By their own efforts, and with the help of other group members, they have made a real difference and have overcome big problems in their lives.

In addition, a variation of the 'formula first session task' (de Shazer, 1985) can be given to clients to orient them towards change:

> *Therapist*: Between now and the group starting we would like you to observe, so you can describe to us next time, any positive events or changes that happen that you want to continue to have happen again.

2   Creating goals and preferred futures

Essentially, solution-focused therapy is about helping clients move from problems and unwanted pasts to solutions and preferred futures. All problems can be transformed into goals and all unwanted pasts can be learnt from to create preferred futures. For example, if a client presents with depression after an abusive childhood, the solution-focused therapist is interested in what this client wants from coming to therapy, what they would like to be instead of being depressed and in what way they would like to learn from the past to guide their choice of a future. Such a re-orientation of therapy is not only arguably briefer and more focused, it can also radically alter the nature of the therapeutic relationship as illustrated in Case Example 2.1 below.

Case Example 2.1   The power of goals

Paul was 15 years old when he was referred to me on account of his long recurrent history of joyriding and theft. He was described on his report as having a cynical attitude towards social services and having no remorse about his crimes. When I met Paul for the first time, instead of going over his problem history, we started talking socially about different things he was interested in. I asked him about what work he thought he'd like to do in the future. For some reason Paul took this question seriously, thought for a while and then gave a clear answer: he would like to be an airline pilot. I was surprised by the answer. Paul was poorly educated and barely literate. It was hard to imagine he had the skills to be pilot. But I resisted the temptation to dismiss the idea and suggest a more suitable career, realising that this is probably what usually happened. Instead I asked what attracted him to being a pilot. This opened up a long conversation and he spoke non-stop about the interest he had in planes, stemming back to his childhood. Over the next few meetings, the subject of planes and other vehicles became our dominant discussion. I took seriously his interest in becoming a pilot and we discussed the steps he'd have to take to move towards this career, for example returning to education. We negotiated a goal of him gaining an apprenticeship as a mechanic, which he achieved within the next two months. When my work with him ended he was working happily in this position. He still spoke of wanting to work with planes, though he had now modified his goal to working as a mechanic with them.

The above case illustrates how much energy and motivation for change can be released when we identify client-centred goals, as opposed to those imposed from the outside or formulated from problem descriptions. Large, idealistic goals, which are important to clients, are highly motivating. Once these are understood and supported, 'small' focused goals, which are realistic in a therapeutic contract, can be negotiated. Once Paul's desire to be a pilot was validated and supported, the more realistic goal of an apprenticeship could be negotiated. Coincidentally, this satisfied many of the referrer's goals since, working as a mechanic, Paul did not commit crime. Most importantly, this was a goal that motivated him and one he was willing to work hard for to achieve in the short term.

In constructing well-formed goals with clients it is important to be sensitive and validate their goals even if they appear unrealistic. Often therapists can inadvertently criticise and put down a client's goal, which can reduce the level of cooperation. As in the above case example, by understanding and validating a client's goal, power and motivation for change can be released. Consider in the next two sequences, taken from a group for children whose parents had separated, how a child's goal of her parents getting back together was handled differently.

Inadvertently criticising client's goal

> *Therapist*: So, say, by coming to this group, good things were to happen, what would those good things be? What would you like to happen?
> *Child*: My parents to be back together again?

Therapist: Hmmh, that may not be possible. You know your Mum and Dad are separated.
Child: I know. (Looks down.)
Therapist: If that is not possible, what would you like instead?
Child: Don't know.

Validating client's goal

Therapist: So, say, by coming to this group, good things were to happen, what would those good things be? What would you like to happen?
Child: My parents to be back together again?
Therapist: You really want your parents to be back together?
Child: Yeah.
Therapist: How would things be different, if that were to happen?
Child: Well I'd see my Dad more and we would all be happier.
Therapist: What are things like when you are happier?
Child: Well there are no rows.
Therapist: What is it like when there are no rows?
Child: Well there are more smiles.
Therapist: I see, more smiles . . . So let's see if I've understood you. By coming to this group, you'd like to see your Dad more and you'd like for everyone to be happier which means you'd like to see more smiles.
Child: Yeah that's it.

In the second example above, though the child's initial goal (her parents reuniting) appeared unrealistic in the context of a therapy group, the therapist respected this and sought to understand the child's motivation better. In doing so, more realistic aspects of the goal were revealed (more contact with her father and people being happier at home), which could be worked on with the child and her parents.

Creating group goals

By bringing together a group of people who have similar or over-lapping goals, extra therapeutic power for change can be released. Feeling a common purpose with other people is highly motivating and supportive, and as certain members make steps towards their goals, a momentum for positive change, which benefits the whole group, can be created. Indeed, it is questionable whether a group can function cohesively unless there is a sufficient sense of a shared task and goal (Johnson & Johnson, 1994).

Thus from the outset, in the design and preparation of groups, it is important to have common group goals, which bring people together and motivate them for change. (This will be considered in detail in Chapter 4.) It is also important to ensure common group goals are highlighted and negotiated on an ongoing basis as the group proceeds. This can be done simply by the facilitator making links between individual member's goals and those of the group, identifying common patterns. Highlighting the similarities between members' goals helps promote cohesiveness in the group. Consider the following example from a men's group in which the therapist identifies links between the different members' goals:

> *Therapist*: What would you like to achieve by coming to the group?
> *Fred*: I would like to be able to hold my cool, especially in work with my boss.
> *Therapist*: Right, I see, that is similar to what Joe [other group member] was saying when he said he wanted to 'keep the head' in work.
> *Joe*: Yeah.
> *Therapist*: So holding your cool or keeping the head are important things for this group to work together on? What does anyone else think?

A goal-oriented group identity

From a solution-focused perspective, groups should be defined in terms of their members' goals rather than their problem pasts, in respect of their strengths rather than their weaknesses. Pride and belief in the group goal is a potent therapeutic factor for change, just as over-identification with the problem can be an inhibiting factor.

Many groups are unsuccessful because they start from a negative and problem-focused identity, which becomes difficult to shift and self-reinforcing for the members of the group. For example this is one of the real dilemmas in forming a group for teenage girls who have attempted suicide. If the group identity becomes centred on suicide and members in the group gain esteem according to their level of suicidal behaviour, then the group could be counter-productive and actually train the participants in more serious versions of their original problems. From a solution-focused perspective, the group could only be successful if its identity was constructed more positively, for example on 'overcoming suicide'. Or it may be best to set up alternative groups centred on different goals altogether such as relaxation groups, assertiveness groups, or general activity and educational groups. Such positively formulated groups are centred on the solution and attempt to answer the basic solution-focused question: 'What will you be doing differently when the problem (e.g. suicide attempts) is completely gone?' For many clients this future will have little to do with the problem and will involve ordinary daily living activities such as enjoying school, making friends, getting on better with parents etc.

Table 2.1 *Comparison of problem and goal-oriented group titles*

Problem identity	Goal-oriented identity
Violent Men's Group	Men Overcoming Violence (MOVE)[1]
Bereaved Parents' Group	Compassionate Friends[1]
Adoption Support Group	Together Expecting a Miracle[1]
Anger Management Group	Just Relax Group[2]
Dieting Group	Taking Off Pounds Sensibly (TOPS)[3]
Divorced Persons' Group	New Beginnings[3]
Heart Surgery Patients' Group	Mending Hearts[3]
Mental Health Patients' Group	GROW[4] Recovery Inc[1]

[1] Yalom (1995)
[2] Schoor (1995)
[3] Schubert and Borkman (1991)
[4] Rappaport et al. (1992)

Many of the self-help group movements, such as GROW for former mental health patients (Rappaport et al., 1992), have long known the power of a positive group identity to bring people together in a shared purpose and to inspire them to reach their goals. It is noteworthy that it is the client-led self-help movement which has generated these positive re-formulations, while professional circles still cling to group identities defined in terms of problems. See Table 2.1 for a comparison list of problem and goal oriented names of a range of actual groups available in different parts of the world.

3 Building on strengths, skills and resources

> There is nothing wrong with you that what is right with you couldn't fix.
> Baruch Shalem

The focus on clients' strengths rather that their weakness, on their resources rather than their deficits, on their competencies and skills rather than their areas of weakness is a fundamental principle in solution-focused therapy. This is not to deny that major problems and difficulties do exist in clients' lives, rather it reflects a central belief that it is more effective, when trying to create change in therapy, to focus on strengths. If clients do create change in their lives or solve problems they do so *out of their strengths and not out of their weaknesses.*

For example, a middle-aged man may become depressed for a variety of reasons: he may have had a recent trauma or loss in his life; he may be having relationship problems with his partner; he may be reliving a childhood pattern of relating; he may be obsessed about negative events in his life. But how this man solves the problem of depression may have little connection with the original causes, but will be generally due to his own strengths and resources. For example:

- He may have the strength of self-awareness to understand the causes of his depression and to distance himself from them.
- He may have the courage to draw on the support of friends and family.
- He may have the persistence to get out and to do things, such as work or engaging in leisure activities.
- He may be able to 'coach himself' and use positive self-talk to overcome negative ruminations.

The solution is ultimately down to his own actions and emerges from within his own strengths and resources. If he receives help such as informal family support in solving the problem, this will be successful only insofar as he is able to avail himself of this support. His ability to relate to his family and draw on their support is a critical variable. Even in the case of formal help such as counselling, this only works with his co-operation and ability to make the counselling work for him. Thus collaborating with clients' strengths and aspirations is the most likely route to success.

In addition, focusing on strengths has a significant impact on creating positive collaboration between therapist and client. If therapists focus on problems and deficits in clients' lives, or conceive of their role as a 'detective of pathology' (Yalom, 1995), then clients will either 'resist' such pejorative descriptions or, if they accept them, their self-esteem is damaged and their ability (i.e. their strengths) to find their own solutions is undermined. When therapists hold genuinely constructive views of their clients, assuming positive intentions and looking out for client strengths (while being sensitively aware of deficits and problems), the context for positive collaboration is established. This is especially the case in brief therapy where a working relationship has to be established quickly.

Many therapists wonder whether this constructive, strengths-based view is possible in very difficult contexts where the client seems to possess few strengths or worse still is actively abusive of other people. A strengths-based view is especially important in these situations. In fact the best way to create change in people who have abused is to establish collaboration with them and to identify strengths which can help them change. Much of the initial research into therapeutic programmes with men who have been sexually or physical abusive of their partners and their children have shown that they have high drop-out and poor outcome (Lee et al., 1997; Shepard, 1992).

However, generally these programmes are deficit-focused and adopt a confrontational rather than a collaborative stance. Given the profile of the client group as having personality problems and a fragile sense of self, they are likely not to respond well to criticism and can experience skills instruction as rejecting (Lee et al., 1997). More recently therapists have adopted more cooperative strengths-based approaches with this client group (Jenkins, 1990; Uken & Sebold, 1996). Jenkins argues that it is ineffective to argue with or confront abusive men about their violence. Rather it is more effective to focus on the strength and courage involved in taking responsibility for violence and to acknowledge any small steps clients have taken in this regard. For example, Jenkins suggests the following questions in the first session:

- Are you sure that you can handle talking about your violence?
- It isn't easy – it takes a lot of courage to face up to the fact that you really hurt someone you love.
- What does it say about you as a man/your strength/guts that you are here today telling me about your violence? (1990: 66)

Even if the man denies the strengths-based description, the therapist can persist and focus on the fact, that even if he was coerced or sent to therapy, some degree of cooperation was necessary on his part.

Come on – a lot of men wouldn't come within one mile of this place, no matter how much they were told or threatened by others – let alone talk about their violence. I've heard of men who sit out in their cars unable to pluck up the courage to enter the building. It must have taken a lot of courage to walk through the door . . . How did you succeed here today? (Jenkins, 1990: 67)

Reframing

Essentially, solution-focused therapy is about thinking differently about problems. The aim is to generate new descriptions about problems in a way that reveals potential solutions. A new description or metaphor can reduce the hold of a problem by highlighting other, healthy aspects of the client's life or by actually revealing a hidden strength or benefit within the problem. When things are seen differently they can become resources in the creation of a solution. This is similar to Milton Erickson's principle of utilisation. As O'Hanlon and Weiner-Davies (1989) state:

Erickson held the view that the therapist should, like a good organic gardener, use everything that the client presented – even things like weeds – as part of the therapy. The 'weeds' of 'resistance' symptoms, rigid beliefs, compulsive behavior, etc., were essential components to be taken into consideration and actively used as part of the solution. (1989: 15)

Reframing is a technique that is used in many different psycho-
therapies from family therapy (Barker, 1992) to brief problem-
focused therapy (Watzlawick, Weakland & Fisch, 1974). In running
cognitive-behavioural therapy groups for depressed clients Scott and
Stradling (1998) suggest the following reframe, which describes
depression as a healthy and necessary time of repair, to be presented
to clients in the first session.

> *Leader*: Depression is rather like blowing a fuse in the nervous
> system, everything goes dead, you feel like a shell, nothing
> tastes the same. It means that you are on strike for better pay
> and conditions, you have a 'Temporarily closed for repair' notice
> on the outside. When you have done the repair job on yourself
> you will open for business again . . . (1998: 142)

There are many different creative ways to reframe problems, the
most important thing is to pick one that fits with the client and
makes sense to them. For example, some clients may not accept the
above reframe of depression as a positive time of repair, especially if
their experience is one of battling with the negative thoughts of
depression. In this instance an alternative reframe such as the
following may be more useful:

> *Leader*: Depression is like a 'black cloud' of negative thoughts,
> which can overcome you. It's a cloud you are trying to keep at
> bay and often you are successful. Often you can ensure the sun
> gets through. In this group we are interested in helping you find
> more ways of 'getting the sun to shine'.

Ideally reframes should emerge from the ebb and flow of the
therapeutic conversation. They should be co-constructed with clients
using their own words and language in order to ensure that they are
useful to them. The best reframes accurately reflect the client's
experience of the problem while adding a new unthought-of angle
which suggests new strengths or possibilities. Consider the following
example of a positive reframe generated within the therapeutic
conversation:

> *Client*: I've felt so low over the last few years. Things got so bad
> that I lost my job.
> *Therapist*: Sounds like your job was important to you.
> *Client*: It was, and it was something I was good at.
> *Therapist*: You were good at it?
> *Client*: Yeah, I've always been a dedicated worker, and a respon-
> sible provider. I always got to work on time and did a decent
> day's work and then ensured there was money on the table for
> my children . . . But in the last few months I haven't been able to

work. I have been too low, and too busy trying to get myself and family sorted.
Therapist: Sounds like you're doing a different type of work now . . . in the last few months you have taken on the very important job of sorting yourself and your family out.
Client: That's right, I need to get things sorted.

In the above reframe, linking in with the client's belief in the importance of work and having a job, his current depressed period is not viewed as being 'out of a job', but rather as having taken on the important new job of getting himself sorted. In this way many of the client's strengths such as being a 'dedicated worker' and 'a responsible provider' are identified and could be drawn upon in gaining a solution to his depression.

Group strengths
Groups can be considered as entities in their own right, with their own identity and character which is distinct from the collective identities of the individual members. The sum is greater than the whole. Even in a newly formed group there is a quickly developing identity and character and in solution-focused groupwork it is useful to identify and emphasise the collective group strengths and skills inherent in the group. For example a facilitator might say:

Therapist: This group really is very honest and truthful in how you all relate to one another.
Therapist: The group shows great support to one another. You can see this by how early some of you arrive to meet one another.
Therapist: There is great warmth and humour in this group despite all the difficulties you have been through.

Such constructive feedback to the group can have the effect of building group cohesion and identifying and mobilising the unique resources within a particular group, making them available to all members.

Groups quickly form their own unique histories. Within the solution-focused approach it can be very powerful to record this from a strengths perspective. This can be done by recording at the end of each session participants' successes, breakthroughs or 'great tips' and collating them in a written summary (or some other ongoing record such as a central flip chart) to be distributed among members. Such summaries can highlight and accentuate progress on a session-by-session basis, and accumulate a wealth of resources and knowledge, which can be drawn upon and referenced at other times.

4   Looking for 'what's right' and 'what's working'

Solution-focused therapists are primarily looking for 'what's right' and 'what's working' in clients' lives. They want to get to know their clients as people who have successes, achievements and talents and who have a lot going right for them as well as being afflicted by problems. In this way, how therapists listen to their clients is imbued with a positive, strengths-orientation. This runs counter to traditional approaches to listening. As (Miller et al., 1997: 12) note:

> Unfortunately, much of what has been written about and considered empathic has focused almost exclusively on the therapist's identifying and connecting with the client's negative feelings and personal experiences (e.g. clients' pain or suffering, their despair or feelings of hopelessness, their present difficulties and the history of the complaint). However since client strengths and resources contribute greatly to psychotherapy outcome, we would do well to adopt a broader view of empathy, a view that encompasses the light as well as the dark, the hope as well as the despair, the possibility as well as the pain.

Genuinely and respectfully listening to clients' hopes and aspirations, their strengths and successes, their talents and special abilities, contributes to a powerful empathetic connection, and from a solution-focused perspective is more useful in building the reservoir of resources with which to construct a solution. One of the rituals in the original solution-focused model (de Shazer, 1988) was giving clients a series of compliments after a structured session break as a means of mobilising their positive resources. Some therapists have cautioned against the giving of overt compliments in case it is perceived as forced or contrived (Nylund & Corsiglia, 1994). Chris Iveson argues that what is important about this process is not whether therapists give the compliments or not, but how *it changes the way they listen during the session* (Iveson, 1998). Looking out for potential compliments or strengths to be given at the end of the session causes therapists to focus on 'what's right' as they listen and thus alters the spirit of the therapeutic interview. Consider the following two contrasting examples of therapeutic listening:

A focus on 'what's wrong'

> Therapist: How have things been since we last met?
> Client: A disaster, I went away for the weekend, but when I got back on Sunday there was a terrible scene in the house.
> Therapist: A terrible scene?
> Client: My son threw an awful tantrum, it was terrible.
> Therapist: Sounds pretty awful.
> Client: It was one of the worst evenings of my life.
> Therapist: Mmmh.

Client: I felt like killing him.
Therapist: Things got so bad that, as you say, you felt like killing him.

A focus on 'what's right'

Therapist: How have things been since we last met?
Client: A disaster, I went away for the weekend, but when I got back on Sunday there was a terrible scene in the house.
Therapist: You went away for the weekend?
Client: I went to see my sister.
Therapist: How did it go?
Client: Well it wasn't bad actually. It was nice to see her.
Therapist: What made you go?
Client: After what we discussed last week I decided I needed some time away for myself, you know, away from the kids.
Therapist: I see, you decided it was important to look after yourself.
Client: Yeah that is right . . . That is why I was so annoyed when I got back to a row in the house.
Therapist: I can imagine . . . there you were, coming back after a nice relaxing weekend to suddenly deal with a row.
Client: Yeah that's right . . . When I was away it made me think how much I wanted things to be better at home, between me and Robert.
Therapist: It is really important for you, for things to be better between you and Robert.
Client: Yeah it is really important.

The second example illustrates how a focus on 'what's right' alters how the therapist listens. In his second response the therapist chose to reflect that he had heard that the client had gone away for the weekend, rather than immediately asking about the scene in the house. This released an acknowledgement of a decision in her life (a change) to look after herself (a strength), by visiting her sister (a resource). These three pieces of information reveal aspects of the client's life which are 'working well' for her despite the presence of the problem, and which could be useful in the creation of an enduring solution. Later the client's annoyance at the row was acknowledged by the therapist, but this was coupled with a constructive understanding that it revealed how much she wanted things to be different, thus validating her high level of motivation.

In solution-focused groupwork the aim is to create solution-focused conversation between group members whereby members constructively listen to one another focusing on 'what's right' and 'what's working' in each others' lives rather than simply what's wrong and the problems which brought them to the group. As well as modelling the conversational style in the way in which he/she interacts with the group, the therapist can encourage such a focus by using structured exercises such as Case Example 2.2 below. This can be used at the beginning of a group.

Case Example 2.2   Focusing on what's right – an exercise for counselling groups[1]

Purpose

Often people get caught up with telling 'bad news' or reporting the things that are going wrong in their lives. The purpose of this exercise is to reverse this and to encourage you to tell 'good news' about what is going right in your life. This can be hard to do as we are often not used to speaking about ourselves in a complimentary fashion. It can also be hard for the listener as we are often not used to encouraging people to speak positively. However, it can be very energising and helpful for the speaker to identify good things and to begin to take credit for them. It can also be refreshing for the listener to move to this different focus and to hear about all the good things in the speaker's life.

Methods

In groups of three divide into the roles of listener, speaker and observer. The exercise lasts for five to ten minutes each way. You should repeat the exercise three times, switching roles to ensure each person has had an opportunity in each role.

In the role of speaker

You are to identify something that is going OK in your life at the moment. You might pick something that you enjoy doing, a relationship that is good for you, or something you feel proud of, or something that just went well last week. You should then simply describe to the listener, what is OK and why. You also talk about how you managed to get this good thing happening in your life. What particular qualities do you have that helped this happen? What do these strengths/qualities say about you as a person?

In the role of the listener

You are to listen carefully to your partner. Encourage them to keep speaking about the above topics. To encourage them to elaborate, you can ask questions like:

1   What went well?
2   What pleased you the most?
3   How come this good thing happened? How did you help bring it about?
4   What particular qualities do you have that helped this to happen?
5   What do these strengths/qualities say about you as a person.

In the role of observer

You listen carefully to the process, taking notes if needed, and feed back to both parties at the end; to the listener comment on the listening skills you have observed; to the speaker comment on further strengths you have observed.

[1] A version of this exercise was originally developed by the Brief Therapy Practice in London.

Focusing on 'what works' in groupwork
The focus on 'what's right' and 'what's working' not only applies to how clients and therapists solve problems together, it also applies to how the therapist should approach the therapy process. The group therapist is interested in finding a way of running a group that is successful for the clients and which is effective in helping them reach their goals. The aim is not only to design groups which match client goals but also to facilitate them in a way that 'works' for the clients. To know this, therapists have to both consult clients in the design of the group and constantly evaluate their work by seeking feedback from them about what is working and what is not working. This can be done by posing simple questions at the end of sessions such as:

● What was helpful during this group session?
● What would you like to continue in the next session?
● What would you like done differently?

By the therapist encouraging, listening to and acting on client feedback, a self-reflective loop is established to ensure that the therapy is and remains effective. Chapter 6 considers systematic ways in which the therapist can collect client feedback on a session-by-session basis to ensure the group remains on target.

Case Example 2.3   Finding what works

Sue, an occupational therapist, was working in an adult mental health day centre. Sue decided to run a women's group to meet the needs of the women who attended the centre, many of whom had been in in-patient units in the past for a variety of psychiatric disorders. The first meeting centred on three questions:

● What did the women want to achieve by coming to the group?
● What way did they want the group to be run?
● What qualities and skills could they each bring to the group to make it go well?

During the meeting the women identified that they didn't want just a 'talking group'. They wanted to use the group to get out of the home, have fun, meet new people and learn new practical skills such as jewellery-making, baking, knitting and aromatherapy. (Interestingly they did not identify the goals the referring professionals had set for them, such as learning how to manage anxiety or to form supportive relationships.) When discussing what skills each of them brought, many identified that they already had experience in many of the activities suggested and as a result could co-lead some of the sessions.

After the second session, the therapist spent some group time evaluating progress with the clients. All the women said they enjoyed the activities but they also liked the discussion that took place informally before and afterwards, and wanted more of this in the groups. As a result a formal time was set aside for group discussion and support. The group meetings were divided into two parts: an activity session for 1.5 hours followed by a social break and then an open discussion group.

The discussion group became a very powerful forum for the women who brought real issues that were affecting their lives. At session four, the women positively evaluated the support group and fed back that they valued the therapist's role in leading the group to ensure they kept on track. They contracted for another four sessions with the same format.

5 Being respectfully curious

Person-centred therapists believe that three core attitudes on the part of the therapist are crucial to creating the facilitative climate for therapeutic change. These are genuineness, unconditional positive regard (or acceptance) and empathic understanding (Rogers, 1986). Solution-focused therapy can be conceived as building on these basic core attitudes while adding one other – a sense of respectful curiosity towards the client. When solution-focused therapists listen to clients they are interested in them as people apart from the problem; they are curious about their goals and what they want in their lives and are interested in finding more about the strengths and resources they possess which will help them get there. The process has been likened to a 'search for buried treasure' (George, 1998). The therapist joins with the client in a search to uncover hidden talents and resources, which they both believe are present and which will lead them to achieving the client's goals. Whatever attitudes a leader brings to a group are very influential. Members are likely to follow suit. Thus if therapists see their role as identifying pathology or interpreting resistance, then this is the likely way group members will behave towards each other. If on the other hand therapists see their role as identifying strengths, focusing on positive change, then members are likely to relate to each other in this manner also. As (Yalom, 1995: 115) states:

> The leader may by offering a model of non-judgemental acceptance and appreciation of others' strengths as well as their problem areas, help to shape a group that is health-oriented. If, on the other hand, leaders conceive of their role as that of a detective of psychopathology, the group members will follow suit.

Constructive questions
Solution-focused therapists express their respectful curiosity towards clients in how they ask questions. Questions are the main intervention in solution-focused therapy and are designed to be constructive, focused on strengths, resources and goals. Questions are used not to gather information but rather to generate experience and new ideas (Freeman & Combs, 1996). Constructive questions generate new experience about potential solutions and the strengths and capabilities of the client. Think of the difference between the following questions:

- How long have you been depressed? (Likely to be known to client.)
- What would your life be like if you weren't depressed? (Possibly unknown or not 'remembered' by client.)

There are six types of constructive question in solution-focused therapy, which will be described in the following sections. They are summarised in Box 2.2.

Constructive questions

- Goal-setting questions
- Miracle questions
- Exception questions
- Coping questions
- Scaling questions

Box 2.2   *Constructive questions*

GOAL-SETTING QUESTIONS   As stated earlier in the chapter, clear, client-centred and achievable goals are central to brief therapy. Unclear or vague goals can lead to ineffectiveness and invariably make therapy longer term (Berg, 1994). The initial stages of therapy are about moving from a problem statement to an underlying goal. Box 2.3 lists some examples of goal-setting questions.

Goal-setting questions

- What things would you most like to be different by the end of the group?
- What change would make the most difference to your life that you think the group could help you with?
- How will you know that you have achieved everything from the group when it is over?
- Suppose you have reached your goal, what will be different? What will you be doing differently? How will you feel? Who else will notice? What will they notice about you that will tell them that you have achieved your goal?
- What will be the first step towards your goal?
- What will be the first change that will tell you that you are moving towards your goals?

Box 2.3   *Goal-setting questions*

Notice that the questions aim to elicit clear, concrete detail. The more specific the goals the easier they will be to achieve. Also, notice how the questions focus on what the client will be doing differently (as opposed to other people) thus making the goal more achievable. However, creating goals is by no means an easy task. Clients are often clear about what they don't want, for example, not to be depressed, but unclear about what they want instead. They may initially formulate goals which relate to other people's behaviour and which are not directly related to them. It can take some time to construct well-formed goals with clients and this process cannot be rushed. De Shazer has described therapy as two people in a room together trying to find out what 'the hell one of them wants!' Consider the following sequence, in which the therapist helps the client move from a vague goal defined in terms of other people's behaviour to a clear, concrete one over which they have direct influence. The example is taken from a group for family members affected by substance abuse.

Therapist: What would you like to achieve by coming to the group?
Client: I don't know. My partner has started drinking again.
Therapist: I'm sorry about that . . . What way would you like things to be different?
Client: I just wish he'd stop drinking.
Therapist: Suppose he were to stop drinking. What would that be like for you?
Client: It would be great. I wouldn't be worrying each evening, waiting for him to come in.
Therapist: What way would evenings go instead?

Client: [*pause*] I guess things would go a lot smoother . . . He wouldn't be as angry.
Therapist: If things were smoother, what would that be like for you? What way would you be?
Client: I'd be able to get on with my own life.
Therapist: Ah I see, you'd be able to get on with your own life . . . What will you be doing differently when you are able to get on with your own life?
Client: Maybe I'd go out more. I haven't been out with my friends in a while.
Therapist: So let me see if I understand this. By coming to the group you'd like to find ways of making things go smoother for yourself in the evening. This would help you get on with your own life, in particular going out with your friends.

MIRACLE QUESTIONS   The miracle question (Berg, 1991; de Shazer, 1988) is recommended in solution-focused therapy as a way of building a clear, detailed and motivating picture of clients' goals. The standard formula for the question is as follows:

> Imagine when you go to sleep one night a miracle happens and the problems that brought you to therapy completely disappear. As you were asleep you do not know that the miracle has happened. When you wake up what would be the first signs for you that the miracle has happened?

The client(s) are then asked to describe in detail what would be different when this miracle had occurred, what they would see, feel, hear differently and how they and others would act differently. The question is fundamental to individual solution-focused therapy and is often the basis of entire sessions (Berg, 1995). The question can be used in many different ways within a group setting. A simple format is to pose the question to the group describing the rationale behind the question and its importance in achieving concrete, detailed goals. Members are encouraged first to reflect on the question individually (perhaps using pen and paper) and then to discuss the results in pairs before sharing with the group as a whole. The facilitator makes sure to reinforce and highlight the positive, detailed aspects of each person's goal and to make links between common goals, thus building group cohesion. A creative group format of using the miracle question via visualisation is described in Chapter 8.

EXCEPTION QUESTIONS   Central to solution-focused therapy is the belief that there are always exceptions to problems (de Shazer et al., 1986). Problem patterns are never rigidly fixed through time and different situations. There are always times and situations when the problem occurs slightly less or even not at all. Indeed, the fact that a person is aware that there is a problem suggests that he/she is making a comparison to another time or situation when the problem did not exist. For example, a woman who feels depressed only knows this if she has a sense of other times when she was happier.

These exceptions are often forgotten, ignored or considered to be 'flukes'. Solution-focused therapists, however, believe that exceptions deserve the closest attention in therapy. They signify examples of 'micro-solutions' already occurring within clients' experience and ways in which clients have applied existing resources. They can be conceived of as chinks in the armour of the problem. If understood and explored they can be amplified and repeated, ultimately leading to the eventual dismantling of the problem. Examples of exception questions are shown in Box 2.4.

General
- Tell me about the times when (the complaint) does not occur, or occurs less than at other times?

Specific
- When does your partner listen to you?
- Tell me about the days when you wake up more full of life?
- When are the times you manage to get everything done at work?

Variations
- When are the times you have come *closest* to remaining calm when disciplining your child?
- When did you last wake up surprised at how good you feel?
- When have you been about to go on a drinking binge but suddenly something happens and you stop yourself?
- Are there times when you expect yourself to lose your temper but you remember something that calms you down?

Amplifying the exception
- How do you explain to yourself why these times are different?
- How do you achieve that?
- What do you do differently then?
- Who else is involved that notices the difference? What do they say or do? What else?
- What would you have to do or say for this to happen more often? What else would help this to happen?

Box 2.4   *Exception questions*

Like all constructive questions, exception questions work best if they spring from the natural flow of a conversation, rather than the simple generic questions in Box 2.4. Notice in the following conversation how the therapist asks a question about an exception hinted at within the client's narrative.

Client: The weekends are the worst. When I come home from work on Friday, the negative thoughts start getting in at me. And I dread the next two days. That's when I feel really alone.
Therapist: So on Friday when you get home, the problems really start.
Client: Yeah.
Therapist: So presumably before Friday, or mid-week, the problems aren't as strong. Presumably things are slightly better?
Client: I guess so.
Therapist: What is slightly better then?

COPING QUESTIONS   Solution-focused therapy emphasises the competency of clients. Despite having problems clients still have access to a number of strengths and resources, which allow them to survive and manage their lives. These strengths are often forgotten or not fully accessed, and if they can be identified and emphasised they can provide a rich store of resources not only in maintaining the current situation but also in solving the problem. Coping questions are particularly useful for clients who are less optimistic about change, who cannot see exceptions or who see the solution as being outside their control. The questions both acknowledge that the problem is real and formidable while also attempting to highlight what clients are *already* doing to combat and manage the problem. They bring to the attention of the client that despite the problem there are positives in the situation that they can take the credit for. See examples of coping questions in Box 2.5.

Current problem
- How do you cope with the difficulties you are facing?
- What keeps you going?
- How do you manage on a day-to-day basis?
- Who is your greatest support, in dealing with this problem? What do they do that is helpful?
- This problem feels so difficult at the moment yet you still managed to get here today. What got you here?
- Sometimes problems tend to get worse, what do you do that stops your problem worsening?

Past problem
- How did you get through that period?
- Who was your greatest support?
- How did they help?
- How did you manage to solve that problem in the past?
- Other people might have had more difficulty but you managed to survive and get here today. How did you manage to achieve that?

Box 2.5   *Coping questions*

SCALING QUESTIONS   When a client sets a goal it can sometimes seem very remote, or too large to tackle all at once. Scaling questions provide a way of breaking a goal down into small manageable steps that can be carried out in the short term. They also help clients to see the progress they have already made and to focus them creatively on the resources, skills and strengths, which move them towards the solution. Examples of scaling questions are shown in Box 2.6.

Standard
- On a scale of one to ten where ten is where you achieve your goal completely and one is the furthest away you have ever been, where would you place yourself now?
- On a scale of one to ten, where one is the worst things have been and ten is the best, where would you place yourself today?

Follow up
- What makes you think you got that far?
- What things have you done already that got you to this point?
- What do you think will move you one step further on?
- What would be the *first sign* that you had moved one point further on?
- Who would be the first person to notice that you had moved one point on? What would they notice about you?

Box 2.6   *Scaling questions*

Scaling questions can be asked in a myriad of different ways and are one of the more versatile techniques of solution-focused therapy. Scaling questions can be used to rate clients' confidence about change and also to highlight their motivation to change, even if they feel their goal is remote or that they haven't made much progress.

> *Client*: I've been having this depression for years. It started when I was a child. I've never been able to cope.
> *Therapist*: It seems to you at the moment that you are coping with a big, long-term problem.
> *Client*: That's right, I know it's to do with me. I know I have to change, but I just feel I don't know how. I feel so far away from being happy. I can't remember the last time I was happy.
> *Therapist*: You sound pretty motivated, that you really want things to change.
> *Client*: Yeah, I am.
> *Therapist*: On a scale of one to ten, where ten is where you really want things to be different and one is where you don't want to change at all, where would you place yourself?
> *Client*: I would say I am at a nine.

Therapist: Wow, that high. What puts you that high?

Client: Well I can't go on the way I am, I deserve a better life. Also so do my children, they have been through a lot because of me.

Therapist: So you feel you deserve a better life, and you also want things to be better for your children. What else puts you at a nine?

In the above sequence, if the therapist had asked a scaling question about how close the client was to their goal or how confident they were of achieving it, these questions would have led to low ratings. However, by instead scaling the client's motivation, new strengths and powerful motives for change were identified.

6   Creating co-operation and collaboration

A collaborative stance is fundamental to the role of the solution-focused group therapist. The therapist always looks for and assumes a co-operative intent on the part of the client. If there is conflict in the therapeutic process, this is not seen as a manifestation of the client's resistance. Indeed in a seminal article, 'The Death of Resistance', de Shazer (1984) conceived of the concept of resistance as unhelpful in creating co-operation. Rather 'resistance' is seen as a shared process co-created in the therapeutic relationship. Perhaps it is due to a vague goal, or the fact that the therapist has not understood the client's 'unique way of co-operating'. The onus is on therapists to take the lead in 'doing something different' to change this context into a more collaborative one. Rather than by confrontation, this is achieved by looking for strengths in the client's position or for positive intentions and goals with which they can co-operate. Often this is achieved by therapists taking a respectful 'one-down position' in the therapeutic dialogue whereby they assume that clients are the experts in their own lives. These therapists go out of their way to accommodate and understand the clients' opinions and views. This is in direct contrast to the common power difference experienced in counselling and therapy where the therapist is seen as the psychological expert in the client's life and in the process of change. Consider the contrasting approaches in the following example:

A 26-year-old female drug user whom I shall call Paula is consistently late to an outpatient drug treatment group which she had been court ordered to attend. If she fails to attend the group then she will be returned to the court and will be likely to receive a custodial sentence. The therapist has decided something should be done and thus asks the client to an individual meeting with him.

Confrontative stance

> *Client*: Is this meeting about why I've been late to one or two groups?
>
> *Therapist*: Well you've been late to every group. You know the rules about being on time to every group.
>
> *Client*: It's too difficult to get to the group each week. Do you know how far I have to travel?
>
> *Therapist*: Well you knew all this when you signed up.

Co-operative stance

> *Client*: Is this meeting about why I've been late to one or two groups?
>
> *Therapist*: I'm sure you must have a very good reason to be late.
>
> *Client*: Yes I do, I've so much to do. By the time I get to the drugs clinic, then collect the children from school and get them to my mother, I'm in a rush to get to the group.
>
> *Therapist*: You've got a lot of important things to do, being a mother and making sure you get your treatment.
>
> *Client*: Yeah, I do try to get to the group.
>
> *Therapist*: I hear that. Despite all the other things you've got to do you still put in a big effort to get here on time. What makes you do that?
>
> *Client*: Yeah, I know I have to. I want to keep the court off my back . . . I don't want to go back to jail. I want to stay looking after my children.
>
> *Therapist*: You want to stay looking after your children, to keep your family together.
>
> *Client*: That's right.

In the second sequence, rather than directly confronting Paula, the therapist first assumes that there are good reasons for her lateness. This allows Paula's positive goals (keeping her family together) and the steps she has already taken to co-operate with the courts (rushing to the group), to be highlighted. From this more collaborative starting point, the therapist is in a better position to go on to explore how they can work together to ensure better attendance.

Even when there are inconsistencies in the client's story or where it is in conflict with other peoples' version of events (as is often the case in working with drug- and alcohol-using clients), the solution-focused therapist does not directly confront these inconsistencies, but assumes that he/she has not understood well enough to clarify the problem. Many therapists describe this respectful, curious stance as adopting the 'Columbo approach' (Selekman, 1997; Van Bilsen, 1991). The therapist dons the 'incompetent bungling' style of the famous television detective and reveals that he or she is confused by inconsistencies in the client's story. Such a willingness to adopt a 'one-down' position and reveal confused feelings can do much to disarm conflict in the relationship between therapist and client and allow the client to maintain their dignity if they change their version of events. Consider the example below similar to one described by Berg (1999) at a training workshop:

> A young heroin addict is in treatment and urine tests have revealed that he has used cannabis in the preceding week. He vehemently denies this, arguing that the positive test must have been caused by the fact that he was in the presence of people who were smoking cannabis and thus 'passively inhaled'. He is at risk of being thrown out of the group programme because of his denial of the facts. The therapist adopts the following approach which gives the client room to change his story.

> *Therapist:* [*showing a genuine attempt to understand*] I'm a little confused . . . Let's see if you can help me understand: you had a positive test which you think might be caused by passively inhaling cannabis.
> *Client:* That's right.
> *Therapist:* And the doctor is unsure that the test would have picked up passive smoking, that he knows of no other case where this has happened.
> *Client:* It must have been the passive smoking, I don't know of any other explanation.
> *Therapist:* You're not sure of another explanation. Let's think . . . It's very rare that someone would fail the test because of passive smoking, because it's not been recorded in the research literature before. It is important we understand it, because I know how much you want to continue in the programme and how much work you have put in so far . . . Let's see if we can think of other explanations . . .
> *Client:* Unless, I accidentally took a drag of a cigarette that night. You see I don't remember too much.
> *Therapist:* So you might have taken an accidental drag.
> *Client:* I went to the party, very clear that I was going to refuse if drugs were offered and I did do that, but later on, I was a little drunk and I'm not sure what happened.
> *Therapist:* So you went to the party with strong intentions and did resist the offers of drugs, which I imagine must have been hard and taken a lot of strength, but later . . .

7 Using humour and creativity

A common reaction to therapists who, when out socially, reveal their profession is: 'Oh don't you find that hard? Isn't it depressing to be listening to other people's problems all day long?' As a solution-focused therapist you could answer that it *would* be depressing if you were listening to problems all day long. But instead you are listening to how people solve problems, how they overcome adversity and triumph against the odds. This listening gives rise to a very different dynamic.

There is a common perception of counselling and therapy as a serious business. Counsellors are dealing with people weighed down by problems and difficulties and this clearly requires a very serious response. From a solution-focused perspective the serious and heavy response to problem-solving can actually be part of the problem. As Freeman, Epston and Lobovits (1997) argue in their aptly titled book *Playful Approaches to Serious Problems*:

> Problems tend to be grim. If they had a credo it might well be: 'Take us seriously!' After all, serious problems demand to be taken this way, do they not? To the degree that a problem is oppressive, the gravity of our attention and the severity of measures taken to remedy it seem bound to increase. Inviting worry, despair, and hopelessness, weighty problems can immobilise families as well as the people who serve them. We wonder whether it is to the problem's advantage to be taken so seriously. By the same token, is their very existence threatened by humour and playfulness? (1997: 3)

Solution-focused groups can be fun, enjoyable and energetic experiences for members. In fact the role of the therapist is to channel this 'fun' energy into creative solution building. A light, even playful approach, can stimulate creative thinking and harness energy towards solutions. An enjoyable, nurturing group can be liberating for people who are demoralised and oppressed by problems and can give them energy to be creative in the face of them. The group should be at least an exception to the burden of the problem so that the time spent in the group is not a replication of problems but a positive exception to them. This in itself can be powerfully therapeutic. For example, in order to attend an assertiveness group, one mother chose to use her precious, once-a-week babysitter. The evening group was her only 'time to herself', free from the demands of her four children. Thus it was important that this group was an enjoyable and nurturing experience for her as well as therapeutically beneficial.

In addition, humour is one of the most powerful weapons against problems. Many group members find it enormously liberating when they stop taking a problem so seriously and begin to see a humorous side to the dilemmas they face. In groups, the realisation through laughter that many others have the same frailties can lift the burden off group members and free them up to consider solutions. Group laughter can cut through shame, guilt and blame and increase self-acceptance. In addition, shared humour creates alliances and connections between people and thus forges cohesion in a therapeutic group.

A facilitator can create a light therapeutic atmosphere by creating an expectation of this in the design of the group and in the preparation of members. They can also create this environment by modelling a non-defensive attitude to themselves. Being prepared humorously to disclose their own minor frailties in a generous way can be liberating to group members and encourage them to follow suit. Consider the following sequence taken from a parents' group discussing the difficulty of approaching schools about problems:

Peter: [upset] When I went to the meeting at my son's school, I felt they were really getting at me. I found it really intimidating.

Therapist: [with humour] It's hard going into a school meeting, it can make you feel like a pupil, like you're back in school again yourself.

Peter: [smiles] That's it. It was as if I was back in school myself and I had caused all the problems.

Anne: [in a comical way] I know that feeling, the last time I had to go into school over my son. I was answering the questions 'yes sir' when the head was talking. I felt like I was about seven years old. [Group laughter]

Therapist: So it's important to remember what age you are when deal with teachers.

In the above sequence the humour broke the oppression of the problem – a problem which is laughed at or diminished by humour can lose its power. From this new position group members are often freed up to consider solutions. In the above example, the therapist could move on to discuss with the group the best way to work with teachers about their children's problems.

Summary

In this chapter we have outlined seven principles of solution-focused therapy and illustrated how they can be practically applied to group-work (see Box 2.1). We have discussed the importance of focusing on change and possibilities and establishing groups which are driven by goals and preferred futures rather than problems or unwanted pasts. Secondly, we have described the importance of building a construc-tive group culture, which is focused on strengths, skills and resources and a search for 'what's right' and 'what's working' in clients' individual lives and in the group as a whole. We have described the respectful, curious stance which is the hallmark of the solution-focused therapist's approach, focused on building co-operation with clients at all times. Finally, we have noted how solution-focused groups are not always serious or heavy endeavours but can be marked by humour, lightness and creativity, a focus which is often the source of their therapeutic power.

3

The Dynamics of Solution-Focused Groups

> For it is group process that truly powers any therapy group. Group therapists must be careful to protect, sustain and use it for therapeutic value.
>
> Conyne, 1999: 155

> The best way to keep groups moving toward solutions is to learn how to stay on their track, toward their goals, using their skills and abilities.
>
> Metcalf, 1998: 44

By their very nature therapeutic groups give rise to powerful dynamics which shape and influence group members. In a well-functioning solution-focused group these dynamics have been activated and mobilised in a synergistic way to work in harmony with members in the pursuit of their goals. This chapter conceptualises the dynamics of groups from a solution-focused perspective and considers how the facilitator can manage group process to ensure that group members support and coach one another as they move towards their individual and collective goals.

The dynamics of solution-focused groups

At any given time, a therapeutic group can be conceived as operating between the following poles: between solution and problem talk; between group-centred and facilitator-centred interactions; and between client-generated and therapy-generated solutions (see Box 3.1). The solution-focused group therapist attempts to manage group process to ensure that there is appropriate balance between the different poles above. The aim is to ensure that:

1   The group is primarily positive and focused on solution talk.
2   Group members interact directly with one another as well as the facilitator and they assume their part in leading the group.
3   Group members generate their own solutions as opposed to simply taking on board solutions which are 'taught' in the group either as an educational component or inadvertently as they are inherent in the therapeutic model.

Solution talk		Problem talk
What's right, solutions and goals dominate group conversation.	vs.	What's wrong, problems and complaints dominate group conversion.
Group-centred interaction		*Facilitator-centred interaction*
Members relate directly to one another, rather than via the facilitator.	vs.	Members relate primarily to the facilitator rather than to each other.
Client-generated solutions		*Therapy-generated solutions*
Clients generate their own solutions and ideas to their problems.	vs.	Clients follow the ideas input by the facilitator, the psycho-educational part of group, or the therapy model inherent in the group.

Box 3.1   *Managing solution-focused group process*

Solution talk vs. problem talk

A useful distinction in solution-focused therapy is the categorisation of therapeutic conversation as either being problem or solution talk (de Shazer, 1994). Problem talk occurs when the problem or 'what's wrong' is the central focus of the conversation. There is an emphasis on finding a past cause or someone to blame for the present difficulties. The feeling content of the conversation is negative with an emphasis on upset, anger, despair etc. Solution talk occurs when the solution or 'what's wanted' is the central focus of the conversation. There is an emphasis on goals, exceptions and strengths and the feeling content is light, energetic and focused on creativity. The central premise of solution-focused therapy is that, within brief therapy, solution talk is more associated with change; in solution talk clients are more likely to move towards their goals and the therapy is more likely to be focused and brief.

It is important to emphasise that problem talk is not always an undesirable occurrence. It often has the effect of developing a bond and shared understanding between members of the group. As stated in Chapter 1, universality is one of the basic therapeutic factors (Yalom, 1995) and sharing problems can give people the relief that they are 'not the only one'. Secondly, some problem talk can provide motivation for change. Focusing on what we don't want can generate angry feelings, which in turn can be channelled towards change. Thirdly, some problem talk can bring an air of realism to a group, clarifying what is changeable (and thus the subject of goal setting), and what is unchangeable and must be accepted. Problem talk alone, however, is unlikely to create change by itself and can become unhelpful if it is excessive or if it is expressed in terms of blame towards other group members. Under these conditions problems can increase in significance causing a 'sharing of despair', or hostility and conflict can increase leading to group fragmentation.

Thus, from a solution-focused perspective, it is ideal to keep the majority of group time within solution talk. Managing group process can be seen as balancing solution talk against periodic problem talk. A good rule of thumb is that a well-functioning solution-focused group spends 80 per cent of session time in solution talk and the remaining 20 per cent in problem talk. Many difficulties occur in groupwork when this balance gets 'out of kilter'. Either the problem talk takes over leading to a sense to helplessness or conflict and resistance. Or solution talk is excessive and the group narrative becomes unrealistic leading to the group process becoming over-idealistic or 'solution forced' (Nylund & Corsiglia, 1994). Managing these difficulties in group process will be addressed in Chapter 7.

Encouraging solution talk in the group
The principles and techniques of solution-focused therapy, described in previous chapters, could be conceived as ways of leading a group into solution talk. Focusing on goals, exceptions, coping and strengths all lead group members away from a problem to a solution-focus. Aside from techniques, facilitators are most influential in leading groups into solution talk in the way in which they attend to the group process. What facilitators draw attention to in a group and what they ensure gets group time powerfully influences the content and quality of the group process. Much of facilitator attention in a group is non-verbal and often facilitators are unaware of their own impact in shaping group process. For example, to whom the therapist extends warm eye contact is likely to speak next; or the comment at which the therapist nods is given bigger importance and is likely to be taken on board by the group; or a facilitator's gesture of inclusion may draw a silent member into the discussion who previously felt no permission to speak. While therapists may not be happy to consider their art reduced to a set of social reinforcers, there is compelling evidence to suggest that how and what therapists attend to in group process generally increases in significance. As Yalom (1995) states:

> Considerable research documents the efficacy of operant techniques in the shaping of group behaviour. Using these techniques deliberately, one can

reduce silences, or increase personal and group comments, expressions of hostility to the leader or intermember acceptance. (1995: 114)

As a solution-focused therapist the aim is to ensure that solution talk is primarily rewarded in the group. However, this is often more difficult than it appears. Therapists are conditioned to attend to problems and to allow them more attention in a group. Consider the following group event, where the therapist over-attends to problem talk.

Sheila is facilitating a six-week personal development group in a mental health setting with seven participants. It is week three and Sheila asks the group to report back on their use of a positive affirmation exercise, introduced the previous week, in which they had to pick out three things they were pleased about in their lives each day. Bob starts first, saying it went well for him and how he enjoyed making the list each day. Sheila, a little tired, did not make much of this, simply smiling and saying 'Well done Bob'. She then looked around the group and asked for someone else to speak. Susan started speaking slowly, saying she found the exercise 'OK' and that she used it a few times. Before Sheila could explore this, Alice came in forcefully.

Alice: It's no good, I couldn't do it all.
Sheila: Oh, [*perking up to listen*] what happened?
Alice: I just couldn't do it, I tried but I didn't have the time. [*Starting to cry.*]
Sheila: [*leans forward in her seat, with a sympathetic expression on her face*] That's OK, don't worry. Tell me what you did. What went wrong?

Alice ends up getting 15 minutes problem-solving time of the group, during which she continually protests that she would not be able to carry out any of the suggested ideas.

In the above sequence, which type of interaction did the therapist reward? Clearly a problem-focused interaction. Though Bob and Susan reported positive change and had both completed the suggested task, they received only a small amount of group time and little social reinforcement from the facilitator. Because Alice presented a problem, she received more time and a great deal more attention. Notice how the facilitator, Sheila, inadvertently provided this attention, via her leaning forward, her change of tone, and her interested facial expression. As a result a problem-focused norm is being established in the group. It would not be surprising if the following week Bob and Susan both reported problems in order to follow the group norm and gain group time and attention. To counteract this Sheila should take more of an interest in the solutions that are described in the group. She could have explored in greater detail and with greater interest how Bob and Susan carried out the affirmation. This could be of great interest and help to Alice as these are the skills that she is trying to learn. By using her powerful influence as the facilitator Sheila could have helped Alice listen to these solutions by leading the group to providing attention towards Bob and Susan. For example, when Alice came in with her problem talk, Sheila could have responded as follows:

Alice: It's no good, I couldn't do it all.
Sheila: I'm sorry to hear that. But, before you continue, let's finish hearing from Susan, and then we will come back to your point.

Being solution-focused in groups is not about denying that problems exist, it is about ensuring that solutions get more attention in the group discussion. A simple maxim is to *attend to the solution first*. Problems can be returned to later if they are still a problem. Often, by simply attending to the emergent solutions within a group, the problems can be overcome. Consider the following example:

Jim: It's no good, I couldn't do the positive affirmation exercise at all.
Facilitator: I'm sorry to hear that. What does anyone else in the group think? [*Facilitator scans other members of group.*]
Sue: Well I found it very interesting. [*Facilitator turns to give attention to Sue – via eye contact, verbal and non-verbal cues – encouraging her to go on.*] I found it useful to pick out the things I do well for a change. It was a bit of a boost to me.
Facilitator: That's great to hear.
[*Facilitator pauses, continues to give non-verbal attention to Sue.*]
Jim: I guess what I'm saying is that I'm just not used to thinking positive about myself.
Facilitator: [*turns full attention to Jim*] I think you are right. It can be a hard thing to learn if you are not used to it. Is it something you would like to be able to do?
Jim: [*pause*] Yeah, I think so.

In the above dialogue the temptation as a facilitator is to respond to Jim's initial statement with 'What did you find difficult?' However this is a problem-focused question which will certainly lead the group into problem talk. Instead, the facilitator did not immediately respond to Jim, but *first* attended to other people in the group who were successfully applying the idea at home. By crucially *waiting* for Jim's next response, a discussion on goals (i.e. solution talk) was allowed to emerge.

Group-centred interaction vs. facilitator-centred interaction

Just as the conversation in the group can be conceived as alternating between problem and solution talk, the functioning of the group with

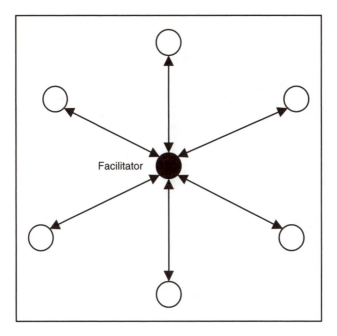

Figure 3.1   *Facilitator-centred interaction*

respect to the facilitator can follow a similar process with the group interaction alternating between facilitator-centred and group-centred. When facilitator-centred, the group members look to the facilitator for leadership and to directly guide the group. Generally when members speak they address their comments directly to the facilitator rather than to the other group members. This communication pattern (see Figure 3.1) generally occurs in new groups when there is a high dependence on the facilitator for guidance and direction. It is also common in structured groups (such as psycho-educational groups), in which there is a high degree of input by the facilitator.

When group-centred interactions dominate group process the members interact directly with each other, rather than in turn via the facilitator at the centre (see Figure 3.2). Members share the group time and take turns between listening and speaking, between supporting and being supported. This is a more mature stage in group process, and requires a degree of trust between group members. Group-centred interaction allows the full power of group dynamics to operate. At this stage members derive powerful peer support and encouragement from each other, and have access to ideas and

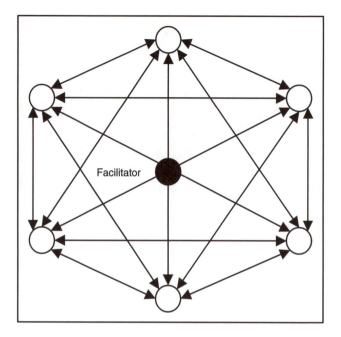

Figure 3.2   *Group-centred interaction*

solutions generated by others. They have now assumed a co-leadership role for the group and take more responsibility to ensure the group fits with their needs and wishes.

From a solution-focused perspective the aim is to ensure most of group time is spent within group-centred solution talk. Group members are encouraged to interact creatively with one another, seeking new ideas and solutions to the problems they are facing. The focus is on celebrating and encouraging small steps and achievements and supporting and 'coaching' one another. The atmosphere is light and energised, focused on creatively finding many different ideas and solutions. The group becomes a motivating factor for members to carry out new ideas and solutions. Group-centred solution talk is often associated with high levels of co-operation and collaboration. The facilitators and group members are working alongside each other searching for solutions to the presenting difficulties.

Encouraging group-centred interaction
There may be periods in which facilitator-centred group process is appropriate and indeed desirable. At the start of a group the

facilitator needs to take control to ensure a common agenda is sufficiently established and that basic boundaries are respected. In addition, in solution-focused groupwork the facilitator has a responsibility to establish a positive solution-focused culture. This is primarily done by taking an active lead in the group and interacting directly with the members in a way that models a solution-focused supportive approach.

However, if the full power of group dynamics are to be activated, then group members must move to a point where they interact directly with one another and assume co-leadership of the group process. It is by listening and being listened to, by supporting and being supported that members have a constructive influence on one another and it is these interactions that give groupwork its thera-peutic power for change. Thus, facilitators have a responsibility to encourage group-centred interaction and 'decentre' themselves from the group process. Facilitators can do this in two important ways: 1) encouraging group support; and 2) encouraging constructive feedback.

ENCOURAGING GROUP SUPPORT   Facilitators can encourage group interaction by simply asking questions that invite members to talk directly with one another. For example, if one member has shared a difficult problem with the group, the facilitator can suggest other people offer support by simply commenting: 'I'm sure other people in the group can identify with that experience' and inviting other people to share. The facilitator can later ask those other members how they solved or coped with the problem and thus generate solu-tions for the original person. Perhaps the simplest way to invoke peer interaction is to open up discussion by asking: 'What does anyone else think?' periodically. Consider the following example, taken from a parenting teenagers group, in which the facilitator draws in other group members encouraging them to support a group member.

> Alice: And then he swore at me. My own son told me to **** off in public. [Starts to cry.]
> Therapist: Ooh, that sounds hurtful. I'm sure other people can understand how that must feel. [The therapist scans the whole group, inviting others non-verbally to contribute.]
> Ger: Yeah, when my teenager swore at me for the first time, I was upset for a week.
> Ann: Yeah, it's so humiliating.
> Alice: And you think you are the only one that this has happened to. That somehow you're to blame.

Ann: You're definitely not the only one. [*There are lots of supportive nods from other group members.*]
Alice: [*smiles*]
Therapist: It's important to realise you're not the only one.

In the above example the therapist activates the therapeutic power of the group by drawing in the other members to acknowledge constructively and support the first client. The support and understanding of fellow clients struggling with similar issues is of great importance and often more powerful than that of the therapist alone. In the next example the therapist goes further to link one member to another, inviting them to communicate directly. Once an empathetic connection is made there is the space in the group to move to consider possible solutions. The therapist goes on to highlight the support and understanding in the group. The following example comes from a group for people coping with depression.

Steve: My wife just doesn't understand how depressed I can get. I think she thinks I should just snap out of it, but I can't.
Therapist: I can imagine that would be hard . . . Someone important not appreciating just how bad things are for you at the moment.
Steve: Yeah.
Therapist: I know other people in the group have talked about similar experiences and about how important it is to be believed. [*The therapist looks at the group members who have had similar experiences, inviting them non-verbally to respond.*]
Ray: [*initially addressing the therapist*] Yeah, I remember when I was in work my boss didn't believe me . . . [*The therapist non-verbally invites Ray to address Steve directly, and this lead is followed.*] Yeah, I remember he thought I was being lazy or avoiding work for no reason. I began to feel really guilty that I couldn't, as you say, snap out of it.
Steve: [*addressing Ray*] That's it. She makes me feel guilty.
Ray: You can't let her, you have to give yourself a break, you know how hard it can get for you.
Steve: [*nods*]
Ray: It's good that you come and tell us about it here. That helped me.
Therapist: So talking about it in this group can help?
Steve: [*addressing the whole group*] Yeah, I guess I know the people here can understand.
Therapist: So people can understand in this group.

ENCOURAGING CONSTRUCTIVE FEEDBACK In solution-focused groupwork constructive feedback can be conceived as part of an ongoing loop of communication between the clients, their fellow group members and the group facilitator. Clients relate their narrative in the group, the group listen and then provide constructive feedback. This feedback acts like a positive reflective mirror for the client, emphasising strengths, positive intentions and highlighting future possibilities. The aim is for the group to be a constructive, supportive 'cauldron' of new ideas and possibilities for its members, which they both receive from and contribute to.

Constructive feedback within a group can be much more powerful than in individual work. This is the case whether the therapist gives feedback to a client, witnessed by the whole group, or whether group members feedback to one another directly witnessed by the rest of the group. Narrative therapists have described the therapeutic power of an audience (White & Epston, 1990). An audience of significant people can lend weight to a client's new understanding or definition of themselves or can provide great motivation for them to carry out a new course of action. A therapist can encourage constructive feedback in a group by modelling the approach. When a therapist constantly seeks to offer positive understandings and uses constructive questions that identify strengths and resources, group members generally follow suit by interacting with one another in a similar way. However, often this 'role-modelling' is not as easy as it seems as therapists can inadvertently provide critical feedback in their choice of questions. Consider the following contrasting examples of critical and constructive feedback taken from a support group for parents of children who have been sexually abused.

> In the second to last session a mother (Alison) who had been experienced by the facilitator as distant and critical of other members, discloses that she was sexually abused as a child and how she feels this made her unable to trust anyone.

Critical Feedback

> *Therapist*: I'm wondering how it is you didn't say this to the group before.
> *Alison*: Don't know.
> *Therapist*: Perhaps you didn't feel you could trust the group enough.
> *Alison*: Yes, I didn't think people would understand.
> *Therapist*: It's hard for you to trust enough that the group could understand.

Constructive Feedback

> *Therapist*: I want to acknowledge how courageous it is for you to tell the group this, and I think it helps everyone, as a lot of people could feel the same way . . .
> *Jean*: As you know it happened to me also. I felt better when I told everyone.

Alison: Well, I wanted to get it off my chest. It's been something on my mind for sometime and I've been wondering whether to tell it or not to the group.
Therapist: What made you tell the group now?
Alison: I think I know everyone well enough and I feel they can understand.
Therapist: Would you say you are beginning to trust the group?
Alison: Yes, trust, that's it.
Jean: I think it is a good idea to wait until you trust someone enough before you tell them something important like that.

In the first response the therapist focuses on the fact that the client did not tell before and on her lack of trust within the group. This statement is covertly critical and could reflect the therapist's frustration with the fact that Alison held back in previous sessions and the negative effect this had on the group. Such critical feedback could have the effect of closing down further conversation with Alison and focuses the group on the problem (a lack of trust), rather than the solution (learning to trust). In the second response the therapist validates and appreciates the strength it took to tell the group and then explores why Alison chose to disclose to the group now, thus highlighting the *emerging* trust within the group. In this way the group focus is on the solution.

At later stages in groups or when there is a high level of trust, therapists can encourage members to provide personal feedback directly to one another. This can be done simply by asking members to comment on one another's experience by asking questions such as: 'What does anyone else think of how Alison spoke up now in the group?' 'What does it say about the group that she was able to trust everyone enough to speak?' Answers to these questions can provide powerful personal reinforcement to Alison and to the group as a whole, further developing group cohesion and trust. Consider the following example taken from a group for substance users, where the therapist encourages the group members to feedback personally to Joe who has been struggling to control his drinking:

Joe: It's been a real battle for me trying to control my drinking. All weekend I sat in. I didn't go out to the pub, but it was all I thought about.
Therapist: You managed though not to drink, you beat the temptation?
Joe: Yeah, just about.
Therapist: What does anyone else think about how Joe was able to beat the temptation?
Paul: Well, it's pretty good. I know how hard it is when you get the craving like that. And it must be hard for Joe, because he has just quit.

Therapist: So it's quite an achievement because he has just quit [*pause*]. What do you think it says about him that he was able to beat the craving?
Paul: He must really have had some strength to do it.
Therapist: Is that right Joe? You must have some strength to do it.
Joe: I guess.
Therapist: What is this strength, that Paul recognises, that helped you beat the craving?

In the above sequence the facilitator's questions: 'What does anyone else think about how Joe was able to beat the temptation?' and 'What do you think it says about him that he was able to beat the craving?', invited others in the group to comment constructively on Joe's ability to stay off alcohol for the weekend, identifying their perception of his strengths and personal qualities. This feedback can powerfully support Joe and help him access personal resources to 'beat his craving'. We shall see in Chapter 5 how a ritual in the final session of a solution-focused group can provide the opportunity for powerful inter-member feedback which can consolidate change and reinforce gains made.

Client-generated solutions vs. therapy-generated solutions

While the focus in therapeutic groupwork is to help clients make their own decisions and generate their own solutions, the majority of groupwork has some psycho-educational component. It involves directly or indirectly the imparting of prescribed or therapy-generated solutions to clients, whether this is in the form of teaching cognitive techniques to combat depression in CBT groups (e.g. Scott & Stradling, 1998) or providing background information to group members such as giving medical information on schizophrenia to a relatives' support group. Even in strictly therapeutic groups, that have no specific teaching or information input, there is always an implicit psycho-educational component in that clients are taught about and inculcated in the therapeutic model inherent in the group. For example, in a solution-focused group clients are taught about goal setting, exception finding and a strengths-orientation as a way of solving problems, or in a psychodynamic group they are taught about the importance of understanding the past and the origin of problems in order to solve them.

Therefore, in any given group clients have access to both the solutions and ideas they generate themselves and to those imparted by the facilitator either systematically (in the information or 'teaching' provided) or indirectly (in how the facilitator models the therapeutic approach). The role of the facilitator is to ensure there is a balance between the client-generated and therapy-generated solutions. The effectiveness of the group will be severely limited if clients simply 'learn by rote' the suggested ideas or accept the therapeutic model without evaluating it for themselves. Thus the facilitator needs to encourage challenge and debate about the presented ideas and to negotiate the method and content of the group, to ensure that clients assume appropriate leadership and generate solutions for themselves.

Solution-building in psycho-educational groups
In psycho-educational groups specific ideas are introduced to clients about possible ways of solving problems. For example, relaxation exercises may be demonstrated as a means of managing anxiety in a stress management group. Groupwork can offer a more empowering way for psycho-educational input to be provided than within individual work. On a one-to-one basis, the imparting of information can appear hierarchical and didactic and can take away from the normally facilitative therapeutic role of the professional. Secondly, in a group, there is the opportunity for the discussion and debate of presented ideas. Members can feel more empowered to challenge ideas and thus not to take them at face value but to adapt them to their own life situation. Thirdly, in a group setting members have the opportunity to learn from each other. Learning can become a shared collaborative endeavour, each person as well as the facilitator imparting information to the group.

Whatever 'expert' ideas are introduced, clients still need to personalise and adapt the taught ideas to their unique situation. A solution-focused method of group facilitation which emphasises collaborating with clients to generate their own ideas and solutions has much to contribute to this process. From this perspective the psycho-educational input provides a *starting point* for the solution-building process. The input is used to provoke clients into thinking through how the ideas may apply in their own situation, and to generate their own alternatives if they don't. The 'expert' ideas (from cognitive therapy or behaviourism etc.) are placed alongside the ideas generated by the clients in the group discussion with the aim of a finding a solution which fits their unique situation.

Listed below are a number of solution-building techniques, which can start the process of solution building even in a highly structured psycho-educational group (see Box 3.2). These techniques can apply equally well to a training or teaching group, where trainers are trying to balance didactic teaching with drawing and building on students' already existing knowledge.

- Predicting – encouraging clients to come up with ideas first.
- Reviewing – reviewing with clients their views in response to presented ideas.
- Finding fit – helping clients choose the ideas that fit them.
- Planning – helping clients plan how to adapt the ideas at home.

Box 3.2   *Solution building in psycho-educational groups*

PREDICTING   Prior to introducing a new idea or technique, the facilitator first encourages the clients to predict what will be covered, thus validating their knowledge of the topic. This can be done in two ways. Firstly, clients' views can be gained by introducing the topic via a series of preliminary questions. For example, before giving an input on methods of relaxation, the facilitator could first ask the following questions to draw on clients' existing knowledge:

- How important is it to find times to relax?
- What are your favourite ways to relax?
- What makes them work for you?

The facilitator then listens carefully to the clients' responses validating their ideas and suggestions, and looking for connections to the ideas that he or she will be introducing. Making connections to the course material affirms the clients' competency and makes the future input more familiar and relevant.

Clients' knowledge can also be validated in advance, by the facilitator making links to their previous examples of successful solutions which illustrate what will be covered in the subsequent teaching input.

Therapist: We are now going to look at how important it is to find ways to relax each day. This is something that you raised Alice, when you described how you had a good day yesterday because you felt a bit more relaxed. Can you tell us a bit more about this? What made you a bit more relaxed that day?

Alice: I don't know. I think it was that I got up early and went for a walk. Yeah, getting out of the house and into the park, that set me right for the rest of the day.

Therapist: That's interesting Alice, because one of the main ways the book [*referring to course book*] recommends people to relax is for them to build in daily exercise into their routine. Something as simple as walking can make a big difference. This seems to be something that has worked for you.

Alice: Yeah, I know if I walk in the morning that it is going to be a good day.

REVIEWING   When some ideas have been presented to the group, the facilitator encourages clients to share their responses, ideas and judgements. It does not matter whether clients agree or disagree with the ideas being expressed, it is more important that they have an opportunity to reflect and think about what is being presented. The presented input provides an important *starting point* for discussion and can provoke a client into thinking about a concept or idea and how it might apply in their life. Without the input this idea may not have occurred to them. Even if they disagree with the input, the process can help them take a stance and to begin to understand and think about their preferred way of doing things. This thinking, reflecting and learning is the most important process in the group discussion. A facilitator can encourage clients to review presented input critically by inviting them to comment. In the following extract from a group focused on teaching communication skills, the facilitator has just shown the group a video vignette of an argument where one person behaved assertively (according to the idea base of the course) and now invites group members to respond to the material.

> *Therapist*: Do you think the approach shown on video is effective?
> *Rob*: Yeah, he seemed to get his point across and he didn't give in.
> *Therapist*: What is making his approach effective? What specific skills is he using that are working?
> *Alison*: Well, he doesn't lose his head. [*Laughter in group.*]
> *Therapist*: So, he remains calm. Anything else?
> *Rob*: Well, he continues to make the same point. He doesn't let the other guy throw him off his point.
> *Therapist*: That's right, he remains quite focused doesn't he?

FINDING FIT   After reviewing the presented ideas and solutions, clients are encouraged to see how these might or might not fit with their own home situation and their specific goals in coming to the group. It is during this section that differences can be explored and valued. Disagreement or challenge to the presented 'expert' ideas at this stage is considered a group strength. The ensuing discussion can reveal how the presented ideas are not perfect, and that what counts is how clients adapt them to their own individual situation. At this point it is also helpful to explore genuine alternative solutions with clients. 'So you feel you would not be assertive in the way described on the video. What way would you do it? How would you talk in a difficult situation like that to ensure you were heard?' A brainstorm in a group can reveal many creative and genuine suggestions, which the clients can evaluate for themselves.

Such a discussion can provide a levelling within the group, where clients no longer see the 'expert' ideas as being necessarily better than their own but on an equal footing. They can feel empowered to take, leave or adapt ideas depending on how they help them get closer to their goals for the group. Consider the following extract taken from a behaviour management group for parents, where the group objects to the idea presented. Notice how the facilitator, by accepting and understanding this objection, validates their knowledge. He then goes on to explore with the group alternatives which fit with their situation.

The group topic is centred on one of the central principles in behavioural parent training, the 'praise-ignore formula' (Forehand & McMahon, 1981; Webster-Stratton & Herbert, 1994), which encourages parents to go out of their way to praise any examples of their child's good behaviour while largely ignoring their misbehaviour. The facilitator has just illustrated the principle with a video scene, which showed a parent specifically praising her two children for playing quietly together by approaching them and commenting on the fact.

Therapist: So what does anyone think of that scene? Would it work for you?

Julie: I thought it was very over the top. A mother wouldn't go over to praise like that.

Therapist: So you mightn't do it like that. What does anyone else think?

Arthur: If all my children were quiet like that I would be afraid to disturb them.

[*Many of the parents laugh.*]

Sue: I'd be afraid they'd run out and mess around.

Alison: If Tom [*her son*] was as good as that, like a little angel, like we saw on the telly, and I went in and said that to him, he would laugh at me and he'd walk into the kitchen and do something naughty.

Therapist: [*addressing group*] So what you're saying is that if your child is doing something right or behaving well, you would be tempted not to comment on it. You would be worried about interrupting the good behaviour? [*Many people nod in the group.*] That seems to be what people are saying?

[*The therapist does not impose a prescribed solution, but attempts to understand the positive basis to their objection, allowing the space for alternatives to emerge.*]

Julie: There are certain times you can do it and certain times you can't do it.

Therapist: When can you do it, when can you pay attention?

Julie: Well if my children were playing quietly like that I would leave them to their own devices, and wait for them to come to me and say look at this picture I'm drawing. Then I would say that's lovely or great.

Therapist: I see what you mean. So you would follow their lead, you would wait for a good time to give attention.

Julie: Yeah, that's right, I wouldn't go over and interrupt them.

Therapist: That's an important point, waiting for a good time to go over and catch them being good.
[*The therapist explores with this parent her own adapted solution, notably waiting for the right time to give her child positive attention.*]

PLANNING   Generally, psycho-educational groups have a homework component. Clients are encouraged to take away the ideas in the group session and to apply them in their lives the following week. From a solution-focused perspective it is important at the end of each group session to encourage clients to review their personal goals, summarise for themselves the key learning points of the session and to create a plan for the following week. While the course material in a structured group may contain suggestions about homework, this space is essential for clients to adapt and personalise it to their own context. This process can be carried out by the client reflecting on their own, or in discussion in the group or in dialogue with the facilitator and can be introduced as follows:

Therapist: We've covered a lot of good ideas in this session. [*therapist summarises the ideas, particularly emphasising those which were generated by the clients.*] In order to take away some of these good ideas, I would like you now to divide into pairs and discuss what particularly struck you about today's group and to decide what ideas you would like to take away and apply at home. As you're doing that, I will hand out the notes for this session, which contain lots of good ideas for going forward. You can either use these or the ones you come up with in your pair, or perhaps even a combination – whichever you think is best. When you've finished your discussion, then I'll ask you to feed back to the big group, saying what your plan is for next week.

Summary

In this chapter we have conceptualised the dynamics of solution-focused group process as operating between problem and solution talk; between group-centred and facilitator-centred interactions; and between client-generated and therapy-generated solutions. We have discussed how facilitators can activate the therapeutic power of groups to ensure that they remain primarily solution-focused, with members taking leadership, interacting directly with one another and generating their own solutions. We also described a process of solution building for psycho-educational groups, which balances didactic teaching with drawing and building on clients' already existing knowledge. This process gives clients access not only to their own solutions and ideas but also to those of other group members and to the 'expert' ideas and suggestions from the taught material. The final solutions are more likely to be meaningful, relevant and enduring given that the clients were partners in their co-creation. Thus the ideas are likely to be better personalised and better fitting to their unique life situations.

PART II
THE LIFECYCLE OF SOLUTION-FOCUSED GROUPS

4
Getting Groups Started: Design, Preparation and Motivation

Case Example 4.1   A poorly developed and planned group

Jim, a social worker attached to a special school for children with learning disabilities, had been thinking for some time about how to set up a group for the parents of the children attending the school. In his clinical practice he had noted how many of the children exhibited challenging behaviour and many of the parents were struggling to deal with them. This concern was shared by the teachers in the special school. Though believing a short-term structured group to be good intervention, he was a bit daunted at the prospect of organising it, especially given his extensive individual caseload. So it became a project that was delayed and put off. Finally, near the end of term, his manager suggested he get the group going as this was seen by the board of management to be an important service to the school's parents. Jim, realising that there was not much time before the summer, immediately set about organising the group. He wrote to the parents, telling them about the aims of the group and that it would start in two weeks time.

On the first night only five parents attended. Some who attended were unsure about the focus of the group and said they wanted more of a discussion group. At the next session only three parents attended, including a new parent who had missed the first session. This group involved some recapping and going over material. After that session Jim made attempts to get other parents to attend by ringing those for whom he had telephone numbers. Though some promised to come, only two who had attended previously came on the third night. At this point, disillusioned, Jim decided to terminate the group. He made up his mind that groupwork was not what the parents were looking for and decided to continue with his individual work.

Though the above is an extreme example, it illustrates some of difficulties in setting up a group and some of the consequences if the

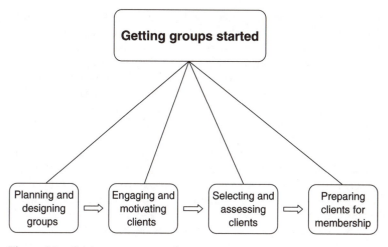

Figure 4.1 *Getting groups started*

group is poorly designed and planned. Though it took Jim many months (from the time he first conceived of the group to the actual running of it) to motivate and prepare himself to run the group he only gave the clients two weeks warning! This put the parents under unnecessary pressure to attend, and himself under pressure to prepare. In addition, Jim did not consult the parents about what they wanted from the group, nor the form of group they thought might help. Essentially, groupwork takes time to design successfully and to set up effectively. Arguably it can require a much higher degree of preparation and planning than individual work alone and can involve negotiation with many other parties other than the client (such as employers, community groups etc.).

This chapter will describe in detail, solution-focused ways of getting groups started and ensuring that they successfully engage and motivate clients, so that they have the best chance of starting and thus finishing well.

Planning and designing groups

Who are the clients?
The key to successful business is quite simple. Find out what the customers want and give it to them. This can be likened to the centrality of client-centred goals in solution-focused therapy that generalises to the group context. Before starting a group, therapists

need to have established clear and positive goals with the clients. However, sometimes even before they can do this they need to have asked an even more basic question: who are the clients?

Most of the time this is straightforward, the clients are the people who enter the counselling office or who enter the clinic door. In other contexts it is less clear, as there are other parties who have an interest in ensuring therapy or treatment proceeds. In the case example above, Jim's employer and the school board of management all had a specific interest in the group proceeding and being successful. This is the case in many other contexts and situations. For example, counsellors working in a drugs agency often have a duty of care not only to the drug users (who may not be motivated to come off drugs), but also to the drug user's family and to the community agencies who are funding the project. Equally, in a child and family clinic, the child and the parents may both be clients to the therapist, even though they may have conflicting goals.

Having multiple clients is not a problem in solution-focused terms, once all their different goals are clarified and common goals and plans established. The aim is to be multi-partial, that is, interested in all the different client goals, thus collaborating with all the different clients or stakeholders in the system. Often professionals are very good at collaborating with the identified client's goals, but less effective at collaborating with the wider system clients, for example the funders of a drugs agency or the school principal who refers children for therapy. Such lack of co-operation can be counter-productive and in the long term does not even serve the interests of the client in the room. For example, if the funders curtail funding or a school principal refers children without proper back-up, then the work with clients is negatively affected. Thus it is important to take a wider view when designing group interventions so that they not only fit with clients' goals but also those of the wider system, such as the community, extended family and professional system.

Type of group
The flexible and practical nature of solution-focused therapy means that it can be applied to a variety of therapeutic groups and contexts as shown in Box 4.1.

In deciding which type of group is applicable to their context, a facilitator should be led by the clients' needs and goals and by what type of group would fit with their context and what is practically manageable. Generally the design of a group should be as far as possible a collaborative exercise with clients to ensure that they are involved from the beginning. Box 4.2 shows a set of criteria which can guide a prospective facilitator in this decision. As we shall see

- *Single session groups*   In some settings such as acute psychiatric inpatient hospitals, client turnover can be so high that facilitators plan each group session as if it is the only session available. (Vaughn et al., 1996) describe an inpatient solution-focused group programme which has three groups in a day with the following focal themes of:

1 'Why now' – focused on generating client goals for current admission.
2 'Solutions' – focused on helping clients develop solutions to current problems.
3 'Choices' – focused on developing client maintenance plans for outside hospital.

The one-day programme is designed to be contained in itself, without an expectation that clients have to complete ongoing groups.
- *Planned short-term and topic-focused groups*   These solution-focused groups are planned to last a defined number of sessions (usually between four and eight); are structured around solution-focused exercises (such as the miracle question, or 'formula first session task' (de Shazer, 1985)) and have an homogenous client group (for example, solution-oriented parenting groups (Selekman, 1993), groups for perpetrators of domestic violence (Uken & Sebold, 1996) or groups in schools (LaFontain et al., 1995).
- *Integrated solution-focused groups*   These groups are generally brief (eight to twelve sessions) and combine structured input from other therapeutic models, such as cognitive-behaviour therapy, with a solution-focused group process. Examples include anger management groups (Schoor, 1997) and parent training groups (Sharry, 1999).
- *Teaching/training groups*   Solution-focused techniques can also be used in teaching and training groups to help students generate their own knowledge as well as to appreciate and adapt didactic input (Sharry, in press).
- *Organisational consultancy/team building*   Solution-focused ideas have also been applied to organisational consultancy and team building by Furman and Ahola (1997) and named 'reteaming'.

Box 4.1   *Types of solution-focused groups*

later these criteria also apply to the selection and assessment of prospective clients for a group.

Duration of group
Solution-focused therapy is primarily a brief intervention. The aim is to be time-sensitive, making the best use of the time available and reaching resolution of the problem that brought the client to therapy

- Agreement on goals: pick a group that fits with client goals and other interested party goals (for example, the organising agency).
- Agreement on method: pick a group format that fits with clients' ideas about how change comes about and culturally matches their expectations.
- Group cohesion: pick group members who will be able to gel and work together efficiently.
- High hope and expectation: pick a group format and 'pitch' that elicits great expectations about the group to ensure optimism about the group's impact is maximised.

Box 4.2   *Criteria for designing a group*

in as short a time as possible. Therapy is not conceived as providing 'replacement social support' in clients' lives but as a means to help them find adequate support in their existing social relationships and networks or to help them access new supports if these are lacking.

Solution-focused groupwork also aims to be time-sensitive and brief. Groups are planned to last between one and twelve sessions, depending on the context. It is also possible to be creative about the timing of sessions to maximise their impact for clients. For example, instead of five weekly group sessions it may be more applicable to have the sessions take place every two weeks, giving clients more time to implement changes and solve problems from their own resources. Selekman (1993), in the implementation of a six-session parenting group, starts with weekly sessions but often increases the time period between sessions as parents become more *au fait* with the ideas and more reliant on their own abilities.

Using review sessions is another way to use time creatively in brief therapy. Barkham et al. (1999) describe a 'Two plus One' model of brief therapy, whereby clients are given two weekly sessions followed by a review after two months. Reviews can be used in similar ways in groupwork. For example, a four-week group intervention can be offered followed by a two month review. Those clients who at review have made sufficient progress can finish treatment and those who have not can be offered further treatment (either a further course of group sessions or another intervention, depending on 'what works' for this client). Using review sessions in this way incorporates many of the core values of solution-focused therapy. Therapy is seen as providing a 'pivotal reflective space' for clients, but change primarily takes place outside the sessions and with the agency of the client. Though the client is not attending weekly the prospect of the review session can keep them focused on their therapeutic goals and mobilise their own resources to achieve it.

Providing a range of brief groups to clients can form the basis of an alternative model of mental health. Rather than providing traditional open-ended, long-term outpatient groups to clients with mental health problems, a range of brief groups can be on offer to clients. For example, a mental health centre may offer groups on assertiveness skills, anger management, relaxation, relationships, parenting and other creative activities which clients can periodically join depending on their needs and goals at any particular time.

Engaging and motivating clients

While there may be some settings where professionals are inundated with motivated clients knocking on their doors requesting to be part of the specialist group the agency offers, the majority of settings are very different. In private practice, counsellors may only come across a handful of clients who are suitable or interested in a counselling group. Statutory mental health agencies may have many referrals but the clients are reluctant to consider groupwork as an option. Drugs counsellors or child protection workers may also receive many referrals but about clients who are reluctant to attend at all. School counsellors may have a 'captive audience' in children attending the school, but to engage them in a voluntary personal development group is another story. Community workers may think it is a good idea to set up a youth group in an area, but to convince the families that this is a good idea and to engage them in the process is often more difficult.

Before any group can be established whatever its nature, the group members need to be engaged and involved. If a group is not well attended by reasonably well-motivated clients from the beginning, or if attendance is erratic or drops off after the first week, then not only do the missing members lose out but also those who continue to attend are disadvantaged. The group suffers as a whole from erratic or poor attendance on the part of some members (Yalom, 1995). Thus, it is essential to engage and motivate clients from the beginning. As solution-focused ideas emphasise identifying client-centred goals and finding fit with the client's style of co-operation, they have much to contribute to the area of engagement and motivation in groupwork.

Motivation
Motivation is often thought of as something fixed and intrinsic within the client. Many professional reports label clients as 'demotivated' or 'unwilling to change', without any further clarification of what exactly they were demotivated about and why they were unwilling to change. The trouble with such global labels is that they

become self-fulfilling prophecies, can create negative expectations and tell us little about potential solutions. They give little information on what the client is in fact motivated to do, and what they are willing to change in their life. Nor do they suggest what ways a professional could work with this client to create a motivational context. All they say is that in this particular instance the professional intervention was not effective. From a solution-focused perspective we are interested in positive possibilities and what could work with this client, even if it is simply pursuing the opposite course of action described in the report which led to 'demotivation' or 'unwillingness to change'.

As stated in the preface, the philosophy of social constructionism underpins the solution-focused approach. Within this thinking motivation is not conceived as intrinsic or fixed within a client, but as something that occurs in a certain context and in relation to a certain set of people. Clients may be motivated or not about a certain goal in a certain context. Their relationship with the professional(s) may be collaborative and thus a motivating factor or conflictual and thus a demotivating factor.

CUSTOMERS, COMPLAINANTS AND VISITORS   In solution-focused therapy clients can be categorised as either customers, complainants or visitors according to their level of motivation with respect to a specific goal at any given time within a specific therapeutic relationship (Berg & Miller, 1992; de Shazer, 1988).

1   Clients at the *customer* level of motivation are ideal clients. They believe there is a problem, are motivated to solve it and, crucially, believe that their actions are necessary in obtaining the solution. They are generally co-operative in therapy and believe the therapist is on their side and can help them.
2   Clients at the *complainant* level of motivation also believe there is a problem and are often highly motivated for a solution. But they feel powerless to create change as they believe the problem is to do with other people's actions and thus beyond their control. The therapeutic relationship can be conflictual as they often want the therapist to 'do something' on their behalf or to persuade someone else to change.
3   Clients at the *visitor* level of motivation either don't feel the identified problem is an issue for them or they are uninterested in the identified goal of the therapy and thus are not really motivated to work towards it. If they do get to the counsellor's or therapist's office it is generally because they are sent or coerced by a third party.

An example of a complainant is a mother who, very concerned about her son's drug taking, insists he attends counselling. The son in this case, who believes his drug taking is not a problem, could be described as a visitor.

Customers, complainants and visitors are not fixed categories and are constructed within a specific therapeutic context. At any given time they give an indication of how satisfactory the therapeutic contract or goal is and how collaborative is the therapeutic alliance. Thus the categories can change rapidly, as the context is changed. The aim of the therapist is to try and create the conditions that allow the client to move into the customer level of motivation. Complainants and visitors require different approaches if this is to happen. For example, the teenager sent to therapy by his mother to stop him taking drugs could become a customer if the therapy focused on a different goal. He may be not motivated at that point to come off drugs but very motivated to regain his independence from his parents. Equally, the mother in the example can move from being a complainant if she is helped to rediscover her power and influence over her son. She may recall a time she was able to 'get through' to him or when drug taking was not a problem in the family. If these exceptions are identified and she can take some responsibility for them, she is on the road to being a customer.

DEVELOPMENTAL STAGES OF MOTIVATION   Visitor, complainant and customer levels of motivation can be thought of as being developmentally related to each other. Often clients pass through these stages as they solve problems in their lives. They may first be a visitor, having no particular awareness of a problem or of something they want to be different. When such awareness is awakened they may not feel influential in creating change and blame others for their predicament and thus become a complainant. Finally, they can discover their own effectiveness with regard to certain goals and thus become a customer. In the example of the drug-using son above: from being a visitor he may become a complainant about his mother pressurising him and restricting his independence, blaming her excessive nagging and controlling behaviour. However, he may finally be able to discover his own effectiveness by being able to communicate to his mother, take on board her concerns and convince her of his need for independence. He is now a customer. Any effective service needs to be able to work with clients whatever level of motivation they have and adapt the approach accordingly.

Visitor, complainant and customer levels of motivation have links to 'the stages of change' model developed by Prochaska, DiClemente and their associates (Prochaska & DiClemente, 1992; Prochaska,

Table 4.1   *Motivation levels*

Solution-focused therapy	Stages of change
Visitor	Precontemplation
Complainant	Contemplation
Customer	Preparation
	Action
	Maintenance
	Termination

DiClemente, & Norcross, 1992) who proposed six stages of change as follows: 1) precontemplation; 2) contemplation; 3) preparation; 4) action; 5) maintenance; and 6) termination. Visitor and complainant levels of motivation roughly correspond to precontemplation and contemplation respectively, while the four latter stages relate to different types of customer interactions (see Table 4.1).

Visitors and complainants are the two types of 'difficult cases' presented by groupworkers in supervision. The difficulty usually flows from the fact that the clients are being treated as if they were customers when in fact they are at a more preliminary stage of change. Whereas group members at the complainant level of motivation are experienced as difficult by being confrontative or challenging to the group facilitator or the other group members, visitors are difficult because they rarely come to the group in the first place or, if they do, remain uninvolved or passively disruptive. As it is such an important theme Chapter 7 will consider difficulty and stuckness within group sessions arising largely out of complainant interactions. In the current chapter we will concentrate on the important first task of getting clients to come to a group. This is largely the task of engaging visitors and enticing them to become customers.

Engaging visitors – getting clients to attend your group
When setting up any professional service, whether it is a parenting group, outpatient group therapy or an adult education course, prospective participants have to be persuaded to attend. People have to be convinced that what is on offer will be of benefit to them. In this way all clients start out as visitors. (Even if they do arrive as customers this belies the large of amount of preparation already done on the part of the client or the referrer for the client to realise that your service could be of great benefit to them.) In fact an initial 'visitor stance' is a healthy one. It is important that clients, rather than simply taking another's concerns on board or accepting your claims about benefit at face value, investigate for themselves about the possible benefits of your service.

Consider how differently motivated the two clients are in Case Example 4.2 about the same assertiveness group. Think about what ways the context could be changed to better engage the second client.

Case Example 4.2 Different levels of motivation

Ron, a psychologist, had been running assertiveness skills groups for adults with depression problems for many years. To make the groups more accessible he began locating them in the community rather than the mental health clinic. He also advertised them in the local adult education guide in an attempt to include a wider population in the group. Among others, Rob and Sue were two of the potential referrals.

Rob was a thirty-two-year-old salesman who saw the advertisement about the course in the adult education guide. He had felt depressed on occasion during his life but was mainly drawn to the assertiveness skills component which he had heard could make him more effective in sales and thus improve his career prospects. He was also drawn to the course because he had heard of the facilitator Ron and was impressed that he had a PhD, which meant 'he must know what he was talking about'. In addition, the course was run in the local community school where his wife and a number of close friends had attended other adult education courses in the past. His best friend, Gerry, was going to attend a different course on the same evening, so the two of them were going to travel together and make a 'night of it' by visiting the pub afterwards.

Sue was a twenty-three-year-old single parent who had been in contact with the mental health services for many years about her bouts of depression, particularly since the birth of her four-year-old son Jamie. Her GP and Community Psychiatric Nurse (CPN) had told her about the course and suggested she attend. Sue had a difficult relationship with her CPN whom she felt didn't listen to her. Sue felt most of her problems were to do with having little support for minding Jamie who was difficult to handle. The CPN told her that first she had to get help for herself and attend this course. Sue was also unsure about the course as the community centre was quite far away and she had never been there before. She was reluctant to use her precious 'once-a-week babysitter' as she liked to keep this for the weekend. In addition, she was unsure about groups, not knowing what type of people would be there. At the previous group she had attended at the hospital, she felt the people had far more serious problems than herself and she found this upsetting. In addition, she certainly did not want to attend alone and would be embarrassed to ask any of her friends given the 'type of group' it was.

In Case Example 4.2 Rob and Sue are at a very different level of motivation about attending the assertiveness group. Rob is a customer: he has clear, positive goals, which he believes the course will help him to achieve and he is actively deciding to attend. Notice the contextual factors which give rise to this high motivation: he trusts the facilitator, the group has a positive image in his eyes, other people similar to him have attended similar courses, the venue is familiar to him and easy to attend, and he is combining his goal for the course with a social one of a 'night out'. All these factors can give rise to high motivation.

Sue on the other hand is at the visitor level of motivation with respect to attending the group: she does not agree with the course goal and is unsure that it could help her. In addition, there are many contextual factors which make it difficult for her to attend. If these were changed and a different group provided in a different context her motivation might also be very different. Firstly, if the group focused on her personal goals she would be likely to be more interested. This could be her goal of 'managing Jamie better', identified above, or some alternative goal which has not yet been explored with her such as going back to work or making contact with other parents. By understanding and focusing on her goals a context for collaboration is more likely to be established. Secondly, the group could be more appealing to her if it was presented as something positive rather than stigmatising and membership was considered valuable and worth pursuing. Thirdly, she would be more likely to attend if the group membership matched her own cultural background and consisted of people with whom she could identify, for example, a group for single mothers her own age, or a group established in her own community which she could attend with a friend. Finally, the group could be more appealing if her genuine practical difficulties were addressed such as making the venue accessible and providing babysitting if necessary.

- Research what the clients want.
- Sell and promote your group.
- Plan in advance.
- Give choices.
- Don't pathologise/be positive.
- Collaborate with referrers.
- Focus on those clients who can benefit.

Box 4.3   *Engaging visitors – getting clients to attend your group*

RESEARCH WHAT THE CLIENTS WANT   In the commercial world business is focused on the customer. The aim is to track customers' wishes and to seek to meet these. In simple terms, the aim is to find out what customers want and to give it to them. Successful therapeutic and educational services are no exception, though professionals from these arenas often find it difficult to take such a business approach.

The essential thing is to find out what a target client group wants and to adapt the groupwork on offer to fit with this. In the case of clients who traditionally have been visitors to professional services this may mean some substantial changes, as often their goals are different from those originally intended by the group designers, as Case Example 4.3 illustrates.

Case Example 4.3   Finding out the type of group the clients want

A community-based child and family centre was set up to provide services to 'families at risk' in a deprived area. Families who had been repeatedly referred to child protection services due to concerns over neglect were highlighted as those most needing services. Initially the workers had difficulty in motivating these families to attend. They offered parenting groups and 'drop-in' mornings, but very few people took part.

As a result they went out and visited a number of the families to discover what services they thought the family centre should provide. The parents identified a number of educational classes – cooking, knitting and needlework – as things they might be interested in attending. Acting on this feedback, the workers began providing these classes which proved to be very successful. Word spread and more and more families attended. A core parents' group was established in the centre, which welcomed many of the new families who attended, and the workers consulted with them about developing further services. After a year the parents identified that they would like a course on parenting, but one they were involved in setting up and which was not just 'telling them what to do'. The workers supported this genuine innovation and within a short time a successful self-help parenting group was established.

Case Example 4.3 illustrates how powerful it can be to attend to client goals in group design. Even though the goals identified (cooking and knitting classes) were not the overt goals of the agency (child welfare) they indirectly led to them. By attending and learning how to knit or cook the parents were gaining essential support and developing themselves as people, all factors which would directly and indirectly improve the well-being of themselves and their children. This leads to one of the central principles of goal setting: movement towards positive, clear, well-formed goals may lead to a 'ripple effect' in that many other positive changes can happen and other over-lapping and independent goals can be met. In addition, in Case Example 4.3, by following the clients' goals a spirit of co-operation and trust was established which led to the exploration of other needs and goals and the eventual setting up of the parenting group.

So what is the best way to discover what clients want? This can be done in many different ways but always involves the simple principle: ask them! In the above example the workers at the centre went out and visited the families, and later on when the group was established, consulted with the core group of parents who attended the centre. More systematically, clients could be surveyed or interviewed either formally by a research study or informally in a series of consultation groups. Generally in the case of clients at the visitor level of motivation it involves getting out of the office to meet them in their local contexts and where they feel most comfortable. It is important to meet them in contexts that emphasise their strengths. This is the difference between meeting a psychiatric patient in a hospital, where they are at their weakest and dominated by the problem, and meeting them in a non-stigmatised setting, for example, in their home or in a community setting. In these different contexts it is easier to meet the person as distinct from the problem, the person with wishes and goals which the right groupwork intervention might help them achieve.

SELL AND PROMOTE YOUR GROUP   In order to engage clients to attend a group, facilitators have to be prepared to market and promote what the group can offer. In short they have to be good salespeople. Though this is a role that often does not come naturally to counsellors, therapists and other professionals in the caring professions, it does help if group facilitators believe in the benefits of the group and are prepared to communicate this to potential attendees. Belief and optimism on the part of the facilitator are strongly correlated with successful outcome (Snyder et al., 1999). If, as a facilitator, you do not believe in the group you are offering, it is time either to change the format or type of group to one you believe in or to engage in a different intervention.

Miller (1998) uses a shopping metaphor as a way of describing the engagement of clients at the visitor level of motivation. They can be likened to people 'window shopping'; they have not yet decided to buy anything, but are merely viewing what is on offer. Like an effective salesperson, the best way for a therapist to respond to people at this level of motivation is to make sure the products appear attractive and appealing and that they are well advertised showing how they could benefit the potential customers. If visitors voyage tentatively into the shop, a good salesperson does not immediately assume they want to buy something, but is a 'good host', showing what is on offer in the shop, ensuring they have all the information they need. Crucially a good salesperson gives a visitor space and time to decide to buy something.

Getting through exams with ease!

Exams and study can be a stressful business and many students welcome some support in managing them. Following on from the success of last term, a new six-week support group is being established to help students study effectively and to manage stress.

Each week new topics on stress management and effective study strategies will be presented and discussed. The aim is to build on your strengths as a student to find the best way for you to study and manage exam stress.

The atmosphere will be supportive and encouraging. Last term all the students who attended described it as being very helpful to them. As one said: 'The group really helped me get down to study, I was really struggling before I joined. It was also fun and enjoyable – a great night out!'

The group will be run over six Tuesdays from 6–8 p.m., will be facilitated by A.N. Other counsellor at the student welfare service. Some light refreshments will be provided. The group will be limited to eight students from the university so make sure to contact us soon if you want to reserve a place.

Please ring for more details.

Figure 4.2   *A group brochure*

One of the most common ways of promoting the benefits of the group is by using a brochure or information sheet that describes the benefits of membership in advance. The more positive and appealing this is to potential members the more likely it is to be successful. See Figure 4.2 as an example.

It is important to remember that word of mouth is also a powerful way to inform potential members about the group and in the end is perhaps more effective. Think of your own experience, if you were to attend an important event, would a good brochure or word of mouth from a trusted friend be more influential in helping you decide? By informing people directly or indirectly via referrers or other clients you increase the likelihood of people wishing to attend. The more positive the pitch and the more respected the message-giver the more likely it is to be received favourably. For this reason, including ex-graduates in the promotion of a group can be very effective, especially if they are from the same culture and background as the clients you wish to include.

PLAN IN ADVANCE   Potential clients often need a lot of time before they can make a decision to attend a group. Think of your own experience when you are contemplating a major life-changing course of action, whether it is a new course or a change of career or moving house, how long does it take you to make a decision? How much information do you need before making this decision? Clients are no different in contemplating attendance at a group which could have a major impact on their life. Often, this can be a long process, sometimes taking months and maybe years. Many people who eventually attend AA groups have been contemplating such a step for many years. This decision process has to proceed at the client's pace. Whereas encouragement and persuasion can help, be careful not to rush this process with another agenda. Planning in advance and having ongoing groups can help this. If the client is not ready to attend now they can take more time to decide and attend a new group in the future. If a client is forced to attend too early in the decision process this can be counter-productive and cause them and others to have a destructive group experience. This can damage their relationship with professional services and make it less likely for them to attend a group in the future. It thus can be more effective to wait and to go at the clients' decision-making pace, giving them enough time to prepare adequately for attendance.

GIVE CHOICES   The more choices a client has about the service on offer the more possibilities we have for gaining their co-operation. Returning to the shopping metaphor, if you as a customer were to visit a shop with only one item on sale and then encountered a shop assistant who tried to convince you that this item perfectly matched your needs, would you believe him? On the other hand if you visited a well-stocked shop with shelves packed with a variety of goods, and encountered a shop assistant willing to discuss with you which product might best suit your needs, inviting you to try them for size before deciding, is this approach more appealing? This is analogous to presenting services and potential groups to a client. Having other options such as different types of groups, or other treatments (such as individual or family work) or other referral possibilities all take the pressure off the client *having to choose* the only option you have available and thus inadvertently limiting their co-operation. In addition, involving the client in a discussion about tailoring the group to their unique situation or giving them the option to 'try out the group for size' (for example, either by allowing them to attend a trial group or watch a videotape of a previous group) can increase co-operation especially when the client is at visitor level of motivation.

Client choice is a cornerstone of the solution-focused group treatment at the Bruge alcohol project (Isabeart & de Shazer, unpublished paper). Clients on referral to the programme are given the option of a variety of treatments such as family work, individual work etc. In addition clients can choose between group programmes working on controlled drinking or total abstinence, according to what they are motivated to achieve. Such emphasis on client choice and co-operation may account for the high level of success with a client group often seen as difficult to motivate.

DON'T PATHOLOGISE/BE POSITIVE

One need not be sick to get better.

Yalom (1995: 493)

One of the inhibiting factors for clients attending groups is often the perceived stigma and shame attached to attendance. For example, to attend an alcohol treatment group you might have to admit you are an alcoholic, to attend an exam stress group at university may be perceived as being unable to cope, or attending a parenting group at a child and family clinic could mean you are a 'bad parent'. Such negative labels associated with a group can prevent the attendance of many members and indeed can damage the self-esteem of many of those who feel obliged to accept problem descriptions of themselves.

From a solution-focused perspective we are interested in creating a positive group identity. Members do not need to 'have a problem' to come. The parenting group is for good parents who wish to enhance their parenting skills, the alcohol group is for people interested in finding new ways to manage their alcohol use. Members demonstrate responsibility in wanting to attend. This may run against the traditional belief that people have to accept they 'have a problem' before change is possible. In studies there is no link between the identification of a problem, 'I am an alcoholic', for example, and positive outcome, for example, giving up drink (Miller & Rollnick, 1991). Many people give up drinking without accepting a 'problem label'. Creating a more positive identity can attract new group members especially those at the visitor level of motivation. As Yalom (1995) argues, a significant attraction for potential members is the degree of pride attached to membership of a particular group.

Creating a positive group identity in the community, where attendance at the group is seen as valuable and worthwhile by a much wider audience can ensure ongoing recruits for future groups. Many self-help group organisations have achieved such highly respected positions in society, for example, AA, GROW, Recovery, and these have endured over time. Other group movements have achieved a positive profile and huge membership at certain times to later pass away and be replaced by something else. The most dramatic example of this is the encounter group movement which reached its zenith in America in the 1960s and '70s, when it was a well-known social phenomenon, to the situation nowadays in which the movement is hardly mentioned but has been replaced by a plethora of issue-focused, educational, support and self-help groups (Yalom, 1995). The challenge to groupworkers is to find approaches that fit with the current concerns and culture of the client group they are trying to serve.

COLLABORATE WITH REFERRERS   Perhaps the best way to motivate reluctant clients to attend a group is to work with those people in the community who want the person to attend and who might be influential in their participation. This could include referrers, extended family, community leaders etc. For example, rather than working directly with a drug-using adolescent, a counsellor might work with his motivated parents to discuss how they can influence their son to attend a group. Or the facilitator of a parenting group might work collaboratively with the social worker referring a parent about whom there are child protection concerns to discover a positive way to encourage this parent to attend.

FOCUS ON THOSE CLIENTS WHO CAN BENEFIT   At the end of the day we have to be realistic about the limits of a particular group and whom it can and cannot help. For some clients, no matter how the group is tailored or how accessible it is, it still will not meet their needs, or they still will not be motivated to attend. For this reason it is important that we do not focus all our resources on this small number of clients, 'over-chasing' them to attend. As we have seen in Chapter 3, facilitators can inadvertently spend an inordinate amount of time on what is not working in the group process and neglect what is going well. It is important not to make an equivalent error at this pre-group stage. For this reason, while it is important to reach out in creative ways to clients who would not ordinarily access our group, we must not lose sight of the needs of the clients whom we are already accessing. Our focus should primarily be on those clients who are able to access our group and those who are able to benefit from it.

Selecting/assessing clients

Let's suppose that, as a facilitator, you have now designed a group. You have also gained approval from the necessary stakeholders and by advertising and other means gained a large number of possible referrals. Should you now assess each referral as to whether the group is suitable for them and, if so, what is the best way to go about doing this? How do you decide which clients might benefit most from attendance?

There is a general consensus that assessment or screening of clients prior to the start of a group is a crucial step shared by solution-focused (LaFontain, 1999) and other group therapists (Corey, 2000; Yalom, 1995). This recognises the power of a group intervention both for good and, unfortunately, for bad. It is thus important to select group members who will not only benefit from attendance but whose attendance will also benefit (or at least not harm) the other members. Experienced facilitators know that, unlike individual therapy, dropping out from a group can be unhelpful both to the member dropping out and also to the other group members who suffer the instability caused by the loss. If possible, it is better to identify with clients prior to starting whether the group fits with their goals and is suitable for them. An early decision not to attend, with the discussion of other referral possibilities, is generally a better alternative to dropping out. The American Counselling Association (1995) put it in their code of standards and ethics:

> To the extent possible, counsellors select members whose needs and goals are compatible with goals of the group, who will not impede the group process, and whose well-being will not be jeopardised by the group experience. (1995: 9)

Traditionally, research into the assessment and selection of clients for group counselling or therapy has focused on trying to define criteria for exclusion (Corey, 2000; Yalom, 1995). The aim has been to identify which 'client types' drop out or have poor outcomes in traditional group therapy, and this has led to the creation of exclusion lists which include clients with labels such as paranoid, sociopath, hypochondriac etc. (Yalom, 1995). Despite the large investment in the categorisation of disorders notably via DSM-IV and the ICD-10, the standard diagnostic interview has been shown to be of little value in predicting subsequent group behaviour and outcome (Piper, 1994). Further, the reliability of diagnosis especially for milder disorders is very poor, even when carried out by experienced, well-trained clinicians (Perry, 1992). However, from a solution-focused perspective we are more interested in identifying inclusion rather than exclusion criteria, more interested in identifying how professionals can co-operate with marginal groups rather than describing the difficulties in working with them. Rather than a client not being suitable for a particular group it is more of a case of the group not being designed for the client's particular needs. As Yalom (1995: 219) notes: 'Almost all patients . . . will fit into *some* group.' The onus rests on the professional to design a group that fits with the clients they wish to engage.

Traditional assessment has also been an 'expert-centred' process. The clinician would review the case notes, interview the client and then decide whether the client was suitable for groupwork and what type of group. The process of assessment depended on the judgement of the clinician and not that of the client. In addition, the criteria and full result of this judgement was not necessarily shared with the client. Belonging to the social constructionist school of thought, solution-focused assessment is seen as a shared process between client and clinician. The criteria should be transparent and focused on inclusion criteria, with the aim of arriving at a consensus assessment about whether the group is suitable or not.

Criteria for inclusion
Below are four criteria to guide a collaborative and solution-focused approach to the assessment and screening of clients for groupwork. The group brochure should list these particular criteria for inclusion, so clients can view them in advance and begin making their own self-selection process (see Figure 4.2). The criteria are adapted to the group context from the indicators of a quality therapeutic process described by Miller et al. (1997) in their analysis of the common factors of effective psychotherapy.

- Agreement on goals.
- Agreement on method.
- Group cohesion.
- High hope and expectation.

Box 4.4   *Criteria for inclusion in a group*

AGREEMENT ON GOALS   There is a general consensus in the literature that a group cannot really function unless there is some sense of a collective goal or shared task (Johnson & Johnson, 1994). Group goals vary depending on the type of group. For example, in traditional group therapy the goal might be to help members have more satisfactory personal relationships; or in a teaching group the goal might be to help students read; or in a bereavement group the goal might be to help members come to terms with the loss of a loved one. To join a group members must be able to share in this collective goal;

their own personal goals must fit in with the group goal. Their own goals do not have to be identical with the group goal but there must be sufficient overlap and common ground between them. For this reason the goals of the group need to be defined prior to the start. It is essential that there are some pre-formed, well-communicated and targeted goals in order to ensure sufficient convergence among members attending. (It is pointless for someone to come to a poetry class to learn car mechanics!) This may all sound simple but a group will not work for an individual if the group goal does not fit with their own goal. As Yalom (1995: 219) states: 'The overriding consideration is that patients will fail in group therapy if they are unable to participate in the primary task of the group.'

This is why goals are of central importance in solution-focused groupwork and why so much time is spent in trying to establish what it is that clients would like to achieve, even before the group starts to ensure the right type of group is being designed in the first place.

AGREEMENT ON METHOD   All facilitated groups follow a certain theoretical orientation that informs the style of facilitation and creates the group norms. For example, an encounter group emphasises self-disclosure and interpersonal sharing and feedback; a cognitive-behavioural group emphasises the teaching of strategies and skills; a solution-focused group emphasises personal goal setting, a strengths orientation and a focus on change. A person should be considered for a group only if the group method or process fits with what they need and expect. This is an important point as many clients drop out of groups if the method does not fit with their preferred style of group facilitation or is one that does not match their strengths. In a study of 109 patients referred to brief analytic-oriented group therapy, the thirty-three drop-outs were found to be significantly less 'psychologically minded' than the continuers (McCallum, Piper, & Joyce, 1992). 'Psychological mindedness' was measured by asking the patients to view snippets of simulated patient-therapist interaction and then to comment on the process. Rather than considering 'non-psychological mindedness' as a deficit in the patients who dropped out it could be understood as a mismatch of methods. The analytic style of the group did not suit these patients and another group method may have been more useful.

It is thus important for us to be transparent about the method with which we will facilitate our group and recognise the inherent limits and the fact that it will not suit everyone. Early identification of a mismatch is preferable to dropping out and gives the possibility of a more appropriate referral. As Yalom (1995: 219) states:

Almost all patients (there are exceptions) will fit into some group. A secretive, non-psychological minded anorexic patient, for example, is generally a poor candidate for a long-term interactional group, but may be ideal for a homogenous cognitive-behavioural eating disorders group.

Likewise solution-focused groups are not suitable for everyone. A client who does not gel with the strengths-based culture or who cannot articulate a personal goal which they are willing to work on, may be best suited to another intervention at this point in time. As LaFontain (1999: 86) notes: 'the two major characteristics for inclusion in SFT groups are being amenable to changing themselves (rather than attempting to change others) and being able to articulate an attainable goal for themselves.'

A final point to note is that, like clients' goals, their preferred therapeutic method is subject to change. Clients' needs and wishes change over time, as their context changes, so reassessment of the 'ideal type of group' is always necessary.

GROUP COHESION   In individual therapy one of the biggest predictors of a successful outcome is the quality of the therapeutic relationship. Veteran researcher Michael Lambert (1992) estimated that it accounted for 30 per cent of the positive change in psychotherapy outcome and was thus the biggest factor the therapist could directly influence by their approach to the work. Group cohesion is the analogous concept in groupwork, incorporating not only clients' relationships with the group facilitator, but also their relationships with each other and with the group as a whole. Yalom (1995) argues that group cohesion is as important as the therapeutic alliance in individual therapy in ensuring a successful group outcome. In a study of forty patients who completed one year of group therapy, the only client factors found early in the group (session 6) which predicted successful outcome one year later were the patient's general attraction to the group and the patient's general popularity in the group, both aspects of group cohesion (Yalom et al., 1967). Therefore, in bringing clients together for a group it is important to try to ensure they are a group of people who will gel sufficiently to carry out the group task. While this is a very inexact science (it is often a mystery why one set of people can hit it off together and why another will not) there are a few guidelines that can help and have the backing of some research. Central to this is the fact that generally those who drop out of a group, or for whom the group is not a successful experience, are different in important ways from the majority who do complete the group. In short they simply 'do not fit in' with the majority culture of the group, and the group cannot accommodate this difference. As Yalom (1995: 229) argues:

There is experimental evidence that the group deviant [*sic*], compared to other group members, derives less satisfaction from the group, experiences anxiety, is less valued by the group, is less likely to be influenced or benefited by the group, is more likely to be harmed by the group and is far more likely to terminate membership.

We can therefore conclude that a major criterion for inclusion is that the client can feel part of and belong to the group. While differences can be rich and helpful in groupwork, it seems that it is the important core similarities that lead to cohesion. People like to be in groups where they can identify with the other members and thus feel comfortable that their culture and mode of communication will be valued and appreciated. This has important implications for professionals attempting to create groups for marginalised sectors in society. Insisting people join groups that are mainly composed of members and facilitators from cultures and backgrounds different from their own is not likely to work. Even if they do attend, membership could become a problem if the difference is not accommodated and valued by the group. In these instances, it would be more successful to go out and create groups and interventions that reflect the values and culture of the people that the facilitators are hoping will participate. As in Case Example 4.2, rather than inviting a young working-class single mother to a parents' group in a middle-class setting, where the majority of the attendees are older and married, it may be more successful to establish a group within her local community, attended by parents of her own age and background and facilitated by a local community leader. Generally it is a good idea to ensure that a person is 'not the only one' of a particular minority group, such as the only black person, or the only older person, or the only person with a disability. Or, if this is unavoidable, particular steps should be taken to prepare this person to ensure they feel included in the group.

Though homogeneity in group membership is important in creating cohesion, heterogeneity can be important in providing richness and diversity. In solution-focused groupwork, differences allow group members to learn from one another. They can witness a range of coping patterns and ways of solving problems that can open up new possibilities for themselves (LaFontain, 1999). Thus group members need to be similar enough so that members can identify with one another and different enough so that they can learn from one another. Ultimately, in deciding how to constitute a group, we should be led by the clients. We can openly discuss with a prospective client the type of group, the type of membership and the issues of inclusion. It can be a shared decision between facilitator and client about whether this type of group fits with their needs at this particular time.

HIGH HOPE AND EXPECTATION   As stated in Chapter 1, hope for and expectation of change is a crucial precondition for therapeutic change both in individual and group counselling. Researchers have found that on pre-group testing, clients who had high expectations that the group could effect positive change in their lives, were likely to profit most from the group (Lieberman, Yalom, & Miles, 1973). Whether a prospective client believes in the group and expects it to create change in his or her life, is thus a major criteria for inclusion. This hope and expectation can spring from a variety of sources:

• A strong belief in the group goal.
• An attraction to and understanding of the group method.
• A pride in group membership.
• Feeling connected to and identifying with other group members.
• Trust in the facilitator or the organisation that hosts the group.

In deciding, with prospective clients, whether they should attend or not, their hope and expectation are significant factors. If they believe more strongly in a different intervention, such as individual work or a group in a different setting, then referral should be considered for that intervention. Or, if they are unsure about membership and not clear whether it could help them (for example, if they are at complainant or visitor levels of motivation, to use a previous metaphor) then it may be preferable to delay membership of the group. Suggest they think through their doubts and consider alternatives, until such a point that they believe more strongly in the group in question or have made their own decision to attend. In this way the timing of when a client should participate in a group programme is crucial and can have a bearing on outcome.

Preparing clients for membership

Many group theorists strongly recommend that members should be helped to prepare prior to the group starting (Corey, 2000; Yalom, 1995) whether this is in the form of individual preparatory meetings or pre-group meetings for the entire prospective group. In solution-focused therapy no clear distinction is made between assessment and therapy or between preparation and therapy, as therapeutic change starts before the first formal session with the therapist (O'Connell, 1998). In groupwork, the process of co-assessing with clients whether they will benefit or not from group attendance is part of the therapeutic change process. Even if the decision is not to attend, a solution-focused assessment aims to identify the clients' goals and their preferred means of achieving them whether this is by another therapeutic intervention or a course of action within their own resources. Assessment is not simply about deciding whether the group will be helpful or not but is also about deciding what other things are helpful in the client's life.

In brief therapy, it is recognised that therapeutic change is mainly the responsibility of clients and *largely takes place outside* of the therapeutic session. Clients' preparation for a group can start long before their attendance, for instance they could be contemplating a certain goal in their lives long before they hear of the group. When they become aware of the group, it could take them some time before they decide that this group might meet their needs and that they could benefit from attendance. Any professional contact with clients prior to a group aims to increase client motivation and build upon any therapeutic change already taking place in their lives, orienting it towards what will be covered in the group. Preparation of clients can consist of many different stages such as sending an initial flier or brochure, an individual screening meeting, a pre-group meeting or a preliminary telephone call.

Budman and Gurman (1988) describe an innovative format for a pre-group meeting which introduces prospective members to one another, gives them a sample of the group method (for example, a role playing of a typical problem situation followed by members offering possible suggestions) and an opportunity to talk to the leaders. The pre-group meeting both allows clients to assess whether the group will be suitable for them and also helps them prepare for it. Though in brief groupwork there can be a tendency to reduce the amount of member preparation because of apparent time constraints, this can be counter-productive as there is considerable evidence for the benefits of group screening and preparation (Hoyt, 1995). Even in a single-session group some preparation, whether this is in the form of initial literature or a short telephone call or a clear introduction prior to the formal group, can reap benefits in ensuring that members are oriented towards the group process. Yalom (1995) describes a model of groupwork in acute inpatient psychiatry where patient turnover is so rapid that effectively each group session must be managed as a single-session intervention. An essential part of the session protocol is an introductory stage, which orients and prepares members for what is to follow.

While the amount of preparation and the type can vary, there are a number of principles which can inform the practice of client preparation in solution-focused groupwork as follows:

Group goals
During preparation the general goals of the group are explained to clients and they are helped to create their own personal goals for

their attendance. Even if goals have been previously discussed it can be beneficial to return to them, reformulating them with greater detail and more personal appeal. It can be particularly useful to formulate goals with a client within an individual preparatory session, which will be revisited in the first session of the group in a goal-setting exercise. Highlighting early on that personal goals are important orients clients to the fact that their own goals are crucial as are their efforts to move towards them.

Give information on group method
Explaining the solution-focused approach to groups, so clients can weigh up its relative merits, is an important step, particularly when clients have been used to traditional problem-focused forms of intervention. This can divert challenges to group process later in the group. In addition, it is helpful to emphasise the crucial role of the client's own commitment in making the changes they want and also their role in giving to and receiving from the other members in the group. Depending on the context an explanation like the following can be used.

> You will notice that the facilitators will really look for your strengths: what you are doing right rather than what you are doing wrong. Our aim is not to criticise you or put you down but to support you in reaching your goals. We believe that concentrating on your successes at home and identifying the improvements you are making is the best way to get you to your goals. Each week we ask people not only to describe the problems they have had but also their successes and what things went well at home. We believe this change of attitude can be really helpful in creating great change.
>
> Though it will be a fun and enjoyable group over the next few weeks, it can also be hard work. People tend to get out of it what they put in. If you work at things over the next few weeks, it can make a real difference.
>
> The other thing you will notice about the group is how important the contribution of the other members are. People get a lot out of meeting each other and learn a lot from each other. Each of you has a lot to contribute.

Anticipate potential problems
It is important to explore any problems or fears a client may have about attending, whether this is practical such as a lack of childcare or emotional such as fear of talking in groups or worry about how lack of literacy will affect their participation. Exploring these problems early allows the possibility of solutions being generated. In addition, clients may only raise them in an individual interview with the facilitator and not with the group directly.

From a solution-focused perspective it is important not to over-emphasise potential problems and certainly not to list 'all the things that can go wrong' to clients as these could become self-fulfilling prophecies. While taking clients' concerns seriously a realistic optimism that the group will go well on the part of the facilitator should be communicated.

Focus on change
A focus on goals begins the therapeutic process as does a focus on change. It can be really helpful in preparation to highlight any positive changes which have already taken place, and how clients can build upon these. An adaptation of the 'formula first session task' (de Shazer, 1985) can be given to help clients build upon these in advance of the group:

> Between now and when the group starts, you may notice other positive changes or come up with other effective ways of managing the problem. Take a note of these. It can be really helpful to bring these along to share in the group.

Summary

In this chapter I have discussed some solution-focused approaches to planning for and designing the right type of group, engaging and motivating clients to attend, assessing with them whether the group is suitable and preparing them for attendance. To summarise these principles I repeat below the case study at the beginning of the chapter, but this time where the preparation and design was successful.

Case Example 4.4   A well-designed and prepared group

Jim, a social worker attached to a special school for children with learning disabilities, was interested in facilitating a group for the parents of the children attending the school. When he spoke to the parents, many of them shared with him the difficulties they had in managing their children's challenging behaviour and said they would like some support in dealing with this. Jim began preparing the group in September, aiming to have it up and running by the following February. He began speaking informally to the key parties in the school about the group to seek their views. He spoke to his manager, the school principal and the teachers at the team meeting. All expressed support for the project, in particular the teachers as they had witnessed the children's difficult behaviour. Jim asked for support in running the group and one of the teachers volunteered to be a co-facilitator. This was supported by the principal.

Jim then approached the parents' committee attached to the school to consult with them about the format and type of group they wanted. Two of the parents from the committee agreed to help in planning and promoting the group and they formed a small organising committee. Together they decided how long the group should be and how it should be structured. The committee agreed with Jim's suggestion to have a pre-group meeting to which everyone could be invited to hear about the group, get a sense of how it worked and to decide if they wanted to attend. They set dates for the pre-group meeting and the subsequent group and sent a flier to all parents inviting them to attend.

Jim and the committee spent the next few weeks promoting the group, offering individual meetings to any parents who expressed an interest. Jim also made a particular point of meeting the parents who did not ordinarily reply to letters and whom he or the teaching staff thought could benefit from the group. The teaching staff also promoted the group by word of mouth, as did the parents' committee. As a result, a huge expectation and interest developed in the parenting group and thirty-five parents attended the pre-group meeting. To facilitate the large numbers wishing to attend, two groups were run in parallel (with the help of teaching staff and the two parents from the committee who acted as co-facilitators), one in the evening and one during the day. At the end of the six-week groups an ongoing parents' support group was established which met monthly and took responsibility to establish future parenting courses and groups in the school as needed.

5

The Stages of Solution-Focused Groupwork

Most groups are usually designed with a number of sessions in mind and tend to have an overall plan, which gives rise to a different structure for each session. This chapter considers the structure of solution-focused group sessions and how this varies over the lifecycle of a group from the first to the last session and even beyond to follow-up or review sessions. In designing distinct session plans the solution-focused therapist should bear in mind the principle that 'every session is the first and every session is the last' (Walter & Peller, p141). The aim is to ensure that each session is complete and contained in its own right and not necessarily dependent on further sessions. Therefore, the following delineation of a group plan into first, middle and last sessions is not to be taken as a rigid proscription. Indeed many of the elements of the first session (such as goal setting and problem-free talk) apply throughout the lifecycle of the group and many of the themes of the last session (such as consolidation and celebration of change) have relevance from the beginning of the group.

- The first session.
- Middle sessions.
- The last session.
- Review/follow-up sessions.
- Case example 5.1 – a school-based counselling group for children.
- Case example 5.2 – an acute inpatient solution-focused group programme.
- Case example 5.3 – an 'anger management/handling conflict' group.

Box 5.1   *The stages of solution-focused groupwork*

First session

Problem-free talk
Many solution-focused therapists recommend that therapy should start with problem-free talk (George et al., 1990; Walsh, 1997). Problem-free talk occurs when the therapist aims to put clients at their ease by talking about their talents, hobbies and interests – things that are going right in their lives and which do not necessarily have a connection to the problem that has brought them to therapy. The aim is to get to know clients as people and to 'engage with the person rather than the person with the problem' (Walsh, 1997: 5). Problem-free talk can resemble social chitchat, though it has a constructive orientation; a skilled therapist is listening carefully for strengths, skills and resources that can be useful later in solving problems. For example, in a recent case working with a family who were referred on account of the son's out-of-control behaviour, the therapist engaged the father by talking about his work as a carpenter rather than immediately talking about the presenting problem. This conversation revealed that the son also shared a strong interest in his father's work and liked to help him on jobs. This problem-free talk identified a connection between father and son that became central to the eventual solution.

Problem-free talk can be incorporated into groupwork in two ways. Firstly the therapist can structure specific social time either before the group starts or after it ends whereby there is an opportunity for the clients and therapist(s) to interact socially with one another. This can be done simply by scheduling time for refreshments and/or ensuring clients have a waiting place to meet informally either before or after the group. Therapists can join in this informal time and use it as an opportunity to connect individually with the clients and build rapport with them. They can model a constructive, affable conversational style to the other clients, highlighting the constructive orientation of this time. Generally problem-free social time is very important to clients in groups, providing them with support, a sense of solidarity and an opportunity to make individual connections with group members whom they feel most drawn to. In addition, problem-free time can be as important to clients as the main section of the group in generating ideas and solutions. For example, in a recent women's group, during the refreshment break one woman described how she was attending a literacy project in her area. This interested another woman in the group who hitherto had been intimidated about attending. After the discussion both women made an agreement to attend the next project meeting together. This was the start of a supportive friendship which lasted after the group had finished.

Secondly, problem-free talk can be introduced in a systematic way in the form of an initial exercise or icebreaker to start the group session. In the first session it can be incorporated into an intro-ductory 'getting to know each other exercise'. For example, the therapist could ask each client to say their name and to reveal a 'secret talent they have' or a 'hobby they would like to take up'. Such exercises can break the ice in a group and help members get to know one another as people rather than being just defined by the problem. In addition, they can be fun and enjoyable, putting people at their ease and helping the group gel as a whole.

Goal negotiation
As stated throughout this book, creating client-centred goals is one of the cornerstones of solution-focused groupwork, so this should take a prominent position in the first session. Though in a well-prepared group individual group members will already have had screening and preparatory interviews which have included goal setting, the first session provides an opportunity for these goals to be revisited and consolidated and also for members to share common experiences and build collective goals for the group. This is usually a crucial stage for the group in terms of building cohesion, a sense of universality and a collective sense of purpose.

Goal setting in the first session can be done in a number of ways. A simple method, which is open to variation, is as follows:

1   Members can be invited to complete a goal questionnaire (see Figure 5.1).
2   They are then invited to work in pairs to share their goals and to discuss what they would like to get out of coming to the group.
3   Members are then invited to complete a 'group round' – each member speaks in turn, stating their goal for coming to the group. The facilitator has an important role during this round, in helping members frame positive goals, in making links between common goals and drawing in other members appropriately.
4   The facilitator (or a nominated person) records the goals on a flip chart which is put on public display and kept as a reference for subsequent sessions.

Method negotiation
While the type of group and the methods it employs should be clear and negotiated with clients (as far as is possible) when the group is being designed and prepared and thus well in advance of the first session, it is still helpful to revisit this area in the first session. As well as recapping how the group will be run and what method it will be

Name: **Date:**

We are committed to helping you get the most out this group. Filling in this questionnaire will help you to be really clear about your goals and thus help us work together to adapt the course to best suit everyone.

By coming to this group, what are your goals? What would you like to achieve?

Please rate between 1 and 10 how close you are to these goals (where 1 means the furthest away you have been and 10 is where you will have achieved your goal completely).

Goal 1	Goal 2
Far away Achieved 1 2 3 4 5 6 7 8 9 10	Far away Achieved 1 2 3 4 5 6 7 8 9 10

What steps have you already taken towards your goals?

What strengths, skills and resources do you bring to the course to ensure you will achieve these goals?

Figure 5.1   *Initial goal form*

following (such as goal setting, exception finding and solution building), the facilitator has the opportunity during this part of the session to negotiate the ground rules of the group such as confidentiality, respecting different views, listening and speaking in turn. During this discussion it is helpful for the facilitator to adopt a collaborative stance and to make many of the ground rule decisions 'open to negotiation'. While taking a lead in these crucial early stages of the group the facilitator should ask for and encourage feedback about methods employed.

The work of session/group task
Generally in a first session, much more time is taken up with the crucial tasks of introductions, goal setting and method negotiation than will be necessary in subsequent sessions. It is also important to start some of the work of the session or to help the group begin the 'group task'. This will vary depending on the type and content of the group. For example in a strictly solution-focused group this might include exercises in exception finding, or in an integrated solution-focused group the first psycho-educational topic may be introduced (such as relaxation techniques in an anger management group) and these debated and practised by clients.

The therapeutic break
In individual solution-focused therapy a therapeutic break near the end of the session is seen as crucial to the total intervention (Berg & Miller, 1992; de Shazer, 1988). The therapist uses the break as an opportunity to formulate a series of compliments about client strengths, skills and resources and sometimes the suggestion of a task designed to mobilise resources to bring about a solution, which they then feedback to the client. During therapeutic breaks clients can also be invited to reflect upon the session, to think about what was important and to make any decisions about going forward (Sharry et al., in press).

Therapeutic breaks are used in a similar way by solution-focused groupwork therapists such as Campbell and Brasher (1994). They can be used as a punctuation or pause point in the group process, which highlights the nearing end of the group session and gives space to members and the facilitators to evaluate what has happened in the group and to make plans. Creating this reflective pause is an extremely important part of a group in ensuring that key understandings are noted and reinforced and in giving members a chance to make decisions and to have these validated and supported by the other group members. The break can be introduced in the following way:

> Therapist: We're nearing the end of today's meeting so let's take a short break for a few minutes to give you a chance to think about what was important during the group today, what stood out for you and what you would like to take away. You may want also to think about what was helpful about today and also what you might like to be different next time.

In a structured solution-focused group with a psycho-educational component (see Chapter 3), the therapist may give handouts which cover the session material and give suggestions for homework, and ask the clients to consider these over the break and how they might adapt them at home.

Depending on the group dynamics, the therapist can suggest clients spend the break reflecting in pairs or in small groups of three or four. In addition, facilitators may choose to leave the room themselves to give the clients space to reflect and also to consult amongst themselves (or with group observers if any) about the group process, and to prepare constructive feedback and perhaps task suggestions for the group members

Planning/going forward

After the break, clients are encouraged to share what they discussed or thought about during the break. In particular, they are invited to comment on what ideas and thoughts they are taking away from the session and in a psycho-educational group how they have adapted and plan to carry out the suggested tasks and homework. In addition, they can also be invited to feedback constructively to one another and the facilitator about what they valued about people's contributions. It can be a useful exercise to record each group member's response in writing on a flip chart or note pad at this point. Such a technique gives extra importance to the content of the feedback and generates an important record, which can be summarised and sent to group members.

After the break, therapists can also provide constructive feedback, both to the group as a whole and to individual group members. This can include a recap of the positive events, successes and under-standings which have been covered in the session and also the identification of new strengths, not hitherto noticed. If there are observers to the group, they can be invited to participate in this part of the group and add their constructive comments to those of the facilitators. The involvement of this 'audience' can add weight to the message given by the facilitators. Facilitators at this point often suggest tasks for clients to consider over the coming week. In the first session, 'skeleton key' observational tasks such as the formula first session task (de Shazer, 1985) can be useful:

> Between now and the next time we meet we would like you to observe, so you can describe to us next time, what happens in your family that you want to continue to have happen again. (1985: 137)

Finally, if facilitators do provide feedback after the break it is best to let the clients have the last word and to evaluate what they have heard. The therapist can simply ask for final comments or con-clusions or more specifically ask members to comment on what they have heard and in particular on whether any part of it fits with them or makes any sense to them. This is also the time to ask clients to complete session rating forms (see Figure 6.1).

Post-session review
It is good practice for facilitator(s) to schedule a post-session review shortly after the group has finished. Even a facilitator working alone can benefit from setting aside specific 'thinking and planning time' to review the group and this can be helped by involving a third party who agrees to act as a consultant/supervisor to the post-session meetings. The post-session review gives facilitators time to evaluate the group and its effectiveness, taking into account the session rating forms, and other feedback they have received. The facilitators can use the time to identify what has worked and what needs to be different as they plan the structure of the next session. It also gives them time to review how individuals are progressing in the group and whether any of them need to be contacted in the intervening week, or whether they would benefit from specific attention at the next meeting. Finally, the post-session review gives facilitators an opportunity to debrief personally from the session, talking through their own feelings and thoughts, thus taking time to highlight their own learning and to 'care for the carer'.

Case Example 5.1   Session plan for a school-based counselling group for children

(LaFontain & Garner, 1996; LaFontain et al., 1995) have developed a format for a solution-focused group for children and adolescents which can be used by counsellors in a school setting. The format is reproduced below.

Session 1   Forming
- Students introduce themselves and ground rules are established.
- 'Getting to know one another' activity is carried out.
- Students are invited to share what they want to change in their lives.
- Formula first session task: 'This week notice what happens to you that you want to continue to happen'.

Session 2   Establishing goals
- Review of last week's task.
- Miracle question: 'Suppose that tonight while you are asleep there is a miracle and the problem is solved. How would you know? What would you be doing differently?

- Realistic goals: 'Now that we have an idea of what you would like to be different and since miracles aren't likely, what *will you be doing* to get that to happen?
- Students establish a concrete goal for following week on a goal sheet.

Session 3   Keys to solution

- Students share their goals from previous week.
- Skeleton key exercise: counsellor discusses skeleton keys and what they are used for. A link is made to 'skeleton keys' for solutions (de Shazer, 1985) – exceptions, doing things differently etc. – and students are invited to identify what 'skeleton keys' they are using. (To make exercise concrete and fun counsellor can hand out 'foil keys' to each child who is identified as using a key.)
- Counsellor discusses other skeleton keys not identified, such as taking small steps towards goal or pretending solution has occurred etc.
- Students are encouraged to identify further skeleton keys they can use in their lives.

Session 4   Progress towards solution

- Students review their goals and progress.
- Counsellor introduces an 'obstacle course exercise' as a metaphor about making progress, helping students identify and overcome obstacles to change.
- Different tasks are suggested to students depending on where they are at, for example, 'do more of the same' to those who are making progress and 'do something different' to those who feel stuck and without options.

Subsequent sessions

- Subsequent sessions are organised as needed to help students maintain progress and to assist those who are stuck.

Final session

- Students review their goals and progress made towards them.
- Students are encouraged to feedback to one another.
- Achievement is celebrated with a party.

Middle sessions

Reviewing progress/focusing on change

A central focus in the second and subsequent group sessions is on client progress. As (Berg, 1994: 150) states: 'the majority of second and subsequent contacts should begin with the question "What's been better – even a little bit better – since we got together the last time?"' Change can be identified and reinforced using the EARS technique (Berg, 1994), meaning the therapist should first *elicit* examples of progress, then *amplify* and *reinforce*, and finally *start* again with a new example:

1 *Elicit* What has been better? What's different?
2 *Amplify* Who else noticed this change? How did you get the idea to do this?
3 *Reinforce* Wow, that's quite an achievement? How come you were able to do it?
4 *Start over* What else is better? What else is different?

Change can be elicited in groups by the therapist addressing the group as a whole with questions such as: 'How have people got on with their plans last week? Who has noticed changes or things that have been different or better as a result?' It can also be done systematically via a group round, where every member of the group is invited to report back about how they got on the previous week. The advantage of the first way is that it allows the members to take more charge of the group direction and facilitates more member-to-member interaction when the changes are discussed. The advantage of a group round is that it ensures all members get an opportunity to speak and that time is more democratically distributed. A skilled therapist can use a mixture of both approaches, by both letting the group lead in the discussion but also directly drawing in quieter group members by direct questions as necessary.

In an average group weekly reports from members will vary from positive change, to no change and to things being worse. The solution-focused therapist is particularly interested in eliciting, amplifying and reinforcing the descriptions of positive change from the first group. When clients report no change, generally these clients are at the visitor level of motivation (see Chapter 4). In these instances, the therapist can adopt a curious stance and search with the client for more detail about what did in fact happen during the previous week, looking for changes and differences that have not been noticed or reflected upon. If the client does not take up the therapist's lead then it can be best simply to thank them for their report and to move respectfully on to the next client. Clients who report no change can often be influenced most by listening to other people's accounts of change, which can invoke in them a curiosity to follow suit in their own lives.

When clients report that things are worse, this can often indicate that they are at the complainant level of motivation (see Chapter 7). In these instances, the therapist can adopt a constructive listening stance, supporting the client while looking out for examples of coping and resourceful responses. Drawing in other group members to support can be very helpful. Once again, it is important not to get stuck into hearing a problem narrative, *clients who report problems should be given no more time than clients who report change in the group* (as often inadvertently happens, see Chapter 3). Even if the client who reports things as worse has not 'come round' to a solution frame by the end of their report, the facilitator should consider simply acknowledging what they have said, offering support and then moving respectfully on to the next client.

Goal setting
Though goal setting and method negotiation might be more prominent in the first session, they should still remain central to subsequent sessions if the groups are to remain on track. The global goals for the group should act like a compass for the group process and be constantly referred to. It can be useful for the group goals to displayed prominently on a flip chart in the group room and for them to be 'revisited' during each session. Members should be given periodic opportunities to review their goals and to make changes and additions. Over the course of a group members' goals often become more detailed and positive and this in itself can represent substantial progress. For example, a client may move from a general, negatively formulated goal such as 'giving up alcohol' to one that is more specific, positive and meaningful such as 'returning to work as a mechanic' or 'visiting relatives (with whom contact had been lost) once a week'. In reviewing goals, evaluation questionnaires (Figure 5.2) can be very useful. Scaling questions are particularly helpful in charting with clients their progress towards goals. In each session the focus is 'how can you move one point on in the scale towards your goal?'

In addition to keeping group goals central to each session, it is also important to negotiate session goals with group members. Put simply the question becomes: 'What would you like to achieve this session?' or 'What do we need to cover this session so that it will be useful to you?' Even in structured groups with set themes each week, it is crucial to be flexible and to respond to the specific needs of the group that week. Many session goals are generated during the 'review of progress' at the beginning of the session. For example, if several members in a group for people overcoming depression identify lack of support from partners as being a major block to progress, it may well be useful to set some group time aside with the specific goal of 'gaining more support from partners' if members desire this.

Method negotiation
As stated earlier, in a brief group the group method is something that should be negotiated and clear in advance of the group starting. The facilitator should start the first group with a clear model of how they are going to structure the session and generally take a lead in

Name:	Date:	
Since coming to the group please rate where you are now with each of your goals?		
Goal 1	**Goal 2**	

Far away   Achieved
  1 2 3 4 5 6 7 8 9 10
	Far away Achieved
	     1 2 3 4 5 6 7 8 9 10	

What has changed? What progress has been made thus far?		
Any changes/additions to your goals?		
What needs to happen to ensure you continue to move towards your goals?		

Figure 5.2   *Goal review form*

implementing this. However as the group develops and members assume more leadership in the process, it can be helpful to negotiate and alter the running of the group according to the needs and wishes of group members. Much of this feedback is provided in session rating forms (see Figure 6.1) and facilitators should carefully attend to and learn from these.

Some method negotiation is helpful in the middle stages of brief groups. This recognises the different needs of each individual group and encourages members to take a leadership and active role in the group's functioning. This helps ensure the group meets their needs and thus has a positive outcome. Changes to group method which are normally negotiated include decisions about when the break is taken, the start and finish times of the course, whether tea and/or coffee is available at the beginning or end, how much time is spent in group exercises as opposed to group discussion or what handouts or summary are given out at the end.

The work of the session
The work for a particular session can be generated from the review of progress at the beginning. Obstacles to progress can be reframed as

goals to be the subject of this part of the session. For example, if one member has relapsed in his alcohol abstinence, the group can join with him in finding resources and strategies to help him 'get back on track'. If progress has been made the session topic can be generated from the question: 'What needs to happen next to help you move the next step towards your goal?'

In many structured solution-focused groups a different theme or focus is introduced during the middle of the session as a way of moving the group on. For example, Selekman (1993) designed a six-week parenting course, where each session is structured around the following 'solution-focused' themes:

1 Solution-oriented parenting: a new way of viewing and doing.
2 Going for small changes.
3 If it works, don't fix it.
4 If it doesn't work, do something different.
5 Keeping change happening.
6 Celebrating change.

The theme is described by the facilitator each week and backed up by discussion and exercises. The aim is to 'teach' solution-focused methods to problem resolution and then help them apply it to their home situation.

It is during this part of the session that creative techniques and group exercises can be very helpful (see Chapter 8). Procedures such as the miracle question using visualisation, or role play/drama or group brainstorming can be very helpful in providing impetus and energy to the group to move to the next stage of solution building.

Therapeutic break/planning/post-session review
The format of the therapeutic break, planning and review sections of the group follows roughly the same format in subsequent sessions as in the first session which has already been described.

Case Example 5.2   Session plan for an acute inpatient solution-focused group programme

In some settings such as acute psychiatric inpatient hospitals, client turnover can be so high that facilitators have to plan each group session as if it is the only session available (Yalom, 1995). Vaughn et al. (1996) describe an inpatient solution-focused group programme, with three group sessions in a day, that is designed to be contained in itself, without an expectation that clients have to complete ongoing groups. The three daily sessions have the following focal themes:

1 'Why now and the management of why now' – focused on generating client goals for current admission. Questions include:

- What brings you into hospital?
- What are you current stressors and how have you been managing them?
- In order for this hospitalisation to be successful, what will be different by the time you are discharged?

2 'Solutions' – focused on helping clients develop solutions to current problems. Topics include:

- Creation of future-oriented, detailed client goals (for example, using the miracle question).
- Encouraging clients to brainstorm and share coping strategies and solutions around common stressors and problems.
- Helping clients identify change that is already happening (for example, what is better since your admission?)

3 'Choices' – focused on helping clients develop a maintenance plan to take outside hospital. Topics include:

- Helping clients to work together to create their own maintenance plan on discharge from hospital.
- Identifying supports and resources that they have access to outside the hospital (such as family, friends and community resources).
- Constructive feedback, identifying client strengths and progress already made.

Final session

The final session of a solution-focused group aims to celebrate and consolidate new understandings and achievements that have been made by group members, while also helping them make plans beyond the group, which help ensure that any gains are maintained and relapses are prevented.

Group review

Participants are asked to review their goals for the group, considering the changes that have occurred between the first and last sessions. In particular, they are asked to think about what important things they have learnt, what gains have been made towards their goals, and what they have valued about the group generally. This exercise can be facilitated by participants initially completing a final goal review form (see Figure 5.3) before sharing their thoughts with the group as

---

Name: **Date:**

Please rate where you are now with each of your goals?

Goal 1	Goal 2

Far away	Achieved	Far away	Achieved
1 2 3 4 5 6 7 8 9 10		1 2 3 4 5 6 7 8 9 10	

What has changed? What progress has been made?

What is the next step? Would you like any further help/ support from the agency or elsewhere or do you feel things have resolved enough for the moment? Please describe.

Any other comments

Figure 5.3   *Goal review: end of group*

a whole. The power of the exercise can be increased by giving the members the forms in advance of the last meeting, so that they have time to think through at home what changes have occurred. In addition, in advance of the group round, the facilitator can display the group goals that were established at the first session on a flip chart for all to see and reflect upon.

Future supports and plans
In the last session it is also important to help members consider their next steps and to plan for 'life beyond the group'. Simple topic questions might be:

- What can you do to ensure gains/progress is made outside the group?
- What supports can you rely on outside the group?
- What is the next step after the end of the group to ensure you remain on track?
- What further support/help would you like from the agency/clinic to keep you on track? Or do you feel things have resolved themselves sufficiently?

These questions can be included at the end of the final goal review form (see Figure 5.3) which members can complete in advance of the group discussion to give them ample time to think through next steps and what further supports and help they might need. During this discussion clients may identify that they would like a future review meeting to meet again as a group or even that they would like to continue meeting in an ongoing way, with or without the facilitator. From a solution-focused perspective, the transformation of a facilitated group into a self-help group can be a very important development in empowering clients to take action for themselves. Even if such a transformation is not possible it is useful if the facilitator is aware of ongoing support or self-help groups to which clients can refer themselves. Indeed, the facilitator may be working in an agency, which provides a number of further groups and services to clients, and these can be included in the list of future options for group members.

It can be helpful to brainstorm with the group as a whole, supports and resources that they can all access beyond the life of the group. This can be particularly powerful in specific focus groups where there are common concerns. For example, in a group for parents of children with a disability, this brainstorm may identify key sources of information and support in the local community, such as specific playgroups who are accepting of disabled children or helpful local representatives who have campaigned for disabled persons' rights.

Celebration of change
A ritual or ceremony during the last session of a brief group can help reinforce the gains and changes made by individual group members and provide an opportunity for members to constructively feedback to one another. Though there are many variations the exercise can proceed with the following steps:

a   Participants are invited in turn to take 'centre stage' and share with the group what was the main thing they gained/ or achieved from attending the group.
b   After each participant has spoken the other members are invited to give positive personal feedback about the contribution the person has made to the group and what they have valued. The facilitator can model this by going first. Examples of simple though effective feedback are: 'What I valued about you, was how you supported everyone through the hard times' or 'I liked the way you were so persistent, you showed great courage.'

c   At the end, the facilitator(s) can take their turn being 'centre stage' saying what they have valued about the group and how they have personally benefited. Participants then have their opportunity to give personal feedback to the facilitator(s).

The therapeutic power of the exercise can be increased by making the ceremony more dramatic. For example, each participant in recognition of their achievement can be presented with an award (such as a certificate of attendance) after they have spoken and receive a round of applause from the group. Or feedback can be given in alternative creative ways: for example, the participants write constructive messages and comments for each other on cards, which are then presented to the person centre stage. Or, finally, the exercise can be prepared for in advance, thus increasing expectations and involvement and the ceremony can be marked by a group celebration or party.

The feedback ceremony is an extremely potent therapeutic exercise. It gives participants the opportunity to sum up what they have valued or learnt during the group, to give personal feedback to members and the facilitator and generally to bring together and consolidate what the group experience has meant to them, highlighting positive changes and reinforcing new constructive self-definitions.

Case Example 5.3   Session plan for an 'anger management/ handling conflict' group

This is an integrated solution-focused group, which combines psycho-educational input on communication skills and conflict resolution with a solution-focused group process.

Session 1

- Introductory 'getting to know one another' exercises and icebreakers.
- Goal setting and ground rule negotiation.
- Explanation of topic – discussion on the purpose of anger and the effect of conflict in clients' lives. Facilitator introduces some positive reframes about the positive functions of anger and the opportunities involved in conflict resolution.
- Planning – during the following week, clients are encouraged to notice the time they get angry or are involved in conflict, particularly noticing the exceptions, the times they feel positively in control or able to manage conflict well.

Session 2–8

The middle sessions follow roughly the same structure as follows:

- Introduction.
- Review of week – facilitated discussion of how each client got on during the previous week, attending in particular to exceptions to the problem, or times when they were closer to their goals for the group.
- New topic – a new skills topic is introduced over the seven weeks as follows:

  1 Making a connection/building rapport.
  2 Active listening.
  3 Speaking up assertively.
  4 Remaining calm 1 (using relaxation and breathing techniques).
  5 Remaining calm 2 (using positive self talk).
  6 Problem solving – finding good solutions.
  7 Bringing it all together – using all skills learnt in real examples.

- Skills practice – in small groups the clients practise the introduced ideas using exercises and role-play with examples from their own lives.
- Homework/planning – suggested 'homework' is given and in small groups clients plan how they will apply this in their own situation.
- Conclusion and recap.

Session 9 – final session

- Review of course material.
- Review of course goals.
- Planning for what next. What further support is needed to keep on track?
- Award ceremony – to mark achievement thus far.
- Group feedback – each member is given the opportunity to feedback to group and other individuals.
- Close.

Review/follow-up sessions

Offering review or follow-up sessions is generally good practice in groupwork and is particularly pertinent in brief therapy, which recognises that therapeutic change generally occurs outside the therapeutic process, both starting well before the therapy has started and continuing beyond the time it has finished. Indeed, brief therapy particularly highlights pre- and post-therapy change as most important as it is achieved by the client by their own agency and with their own resources, thus making such change more likely to be enduring. The purpose of review sessions to harness this post-session change and to provide a future reflective space where this change can be elicited, amplified and reinforced. Many brief therapies use review sessions in this way such as the 'Two plus One' model (Barkham et al., 1999), whereby clients are given two initial sessions followed by a review session three months later.

In groupwork, review sessions can either be offered individually to clients or a group review session can be offered to the whole group. If there is the time, a combination of individual and group review can be particularly effective. The structure of a group review session incorporates many elements of the middle and last sessions above. A simple format could be as follows:

1   Problem-free talk (allowing time for group members to reconnect).
2   Review of progress (what changes have happened since the last meeting?).
3   Goal/method negotiation for session.
4   Future plans (discussion of what next, for instance, further groups etc.).
5   Close.

Summary

In this chapter we considered the principles of designing a session-by-session plan for a solution-focused group. We described the elements of: 1) the first session; 2) middle sessions; 3) the final session; and 4) review sessions and how these might be distinct in focus and constitution. We emphasised the core similarities between distinct stages of groupwork and the importance of ensuring each session was contained and complete in itself. The ideas were illustrated with case examples of three distinct session plans: 1) a four-to-six-week school-based counselling group for children; 2) an acute inpatient solution-focused daily group programme; and 3) a nine-week 'anger management/ handling conflict' group which integrated solution-focused ideas into a cognitive-behavioural approach.

PART III

MANAGING PROCESS – KEEPING GROUPS SOLUTION-FOCUSED

6

Evaluating Groups: Ensuring They Remain on Target

> The hearts of the group practitioner and the group researcher seem to strive for a different destiny . . . Research prompted by a commitment to objectivity and guided by scientific rigor seems to generate a different essence than practice prompted by human compassion and guided by intuitive creativity.
>
> Stockton and Toth (1999: 448)

Traditionally the disciplines of research and psychotherapy have been conceived as distinct arenas. Therapists have been uninvolved in research, fearing its motives and intrusion into their work, and have been ignorant of the process of research and the results it has generated. Yet this has been at great expense to the effectiveness of their work as many of the methods of research have great relevance to the work of the practitioner in ensuring it remains effective and on target.

This chapter describes an evaluation model for practitioners, based on the work of Duncan and Miller (2000), which can be readily used to evaluate groups on a session-by-session basis. The model is mindful of the results of outcome research about 'what works' in therapy, and employs relevant research methodologies to gain client feedback about whether progress is being made.

Developing a model of evaluation

Groupwork generally lends itself to evaluation. Unlike individual therapy, which is often open-ended, groupwork is usually time-limited and planned. The group therapist usually has a defined first and last session or a planned pre-screening and follow-up interview when measures can be applied and data collected about the effectiveness of the group. Brief group therapists, who have a specific interest in achieving an outcome in a short time frame, should have a particular interest in ongoing evaluation. First, they need to establish goals as soon as possible, then orient the group towards them and, finally, closely monitor progress to ensure that the group remains focused and on track. Evaluation is simply a method of monitoring progress by systematically gaining client and other feedback to ensure progress is being made on a session-by-session basis. Evaluation should provide group therapists with feedback from which they can learn and adapt the group interventions to 'what works' in an ongoing cycle of improvement.

Ongoing evaluation also fits with solution-focused therapy. In reflecting on the development of the original model, de Shazer and Berg (1997) described how it grew out of a naturalistic research project to discover with clients about 'what worked' in brief therapy. This research approach gave rise to the three rules of solution-focused therapy:

1   If it ain't broke, don't fix it.
2   Once you know what works, do more of it.
3   If it doesn't work, don't do it again, do something different.
    (Berg & Miller, 1992)

Ongoing evaluation is simply a method of ensuring you find out what exactly is and is not working and that you have a systematic way of gathering evidence for this. Indeed, as we shall see later, many of the techniques of solution-focused therapy, such as goal setting, scaling, and focusing on small steps, can be helpful in evaluating groupwork.

Duncan and Miller in their book *The Heroic Client* (2000) describe a 'client-directed, outcome-informed' model of evaluating individual therapy to ensure that it remains focused on progress and change and that the client is a full participant in the therapy. Basically, the authors recommend using questionnaires, given to clients during each session, to establish with them whether tangible progress is being made and whether the conditions of effective therapy are present (for example, agreement on goals and method, a good therapeutic alliance, and optimism and hope for change). They recommend questionnaires as opposed to verbal feedback as clients often may not report verbally to the therapist when there are difficulties and questionnaires allow for progress to be recorded over time and compared with other clients and normative samples. This chapter describes a way of adapting their methodology to a group format with the addition of solution-focused goal setting as an additional measure of change.

Measuring outcome

GOAL ATTAINMENT MEASURES   Perhaps the most simple and concrete measure of outcome is initially setting goals with clients and then enquiring, using scaling questions, as to whether they have achieved them or made substantial progress towards them. Given the integral nature of goal setting to solution-focused therapy, such measures should be foremost in the evaluation of a solution-focused group. In Chapter 5, sample initial, review and end-of-group goal forms are provided (see Figures 5.1, 5.2 and 5.3) which can help track clients' progress toward their goals.

STANDARDISED PSYCHOMETRIC QUESTIONNAIRE   Duncan and Miller (2000) recommend using a standardised, psychometric questionnaire each therapy session, which can give a comparable 'objective' score on how well the client is progressing. The advantage of using such a questionnaire is that it should have been validated and tested with a range of clients already and normative samples of average and clinical functioning should be available. These questionnaires are the bread and butter of psychotherapy and psychological research and there are many them available to choose from. Duncan and Miller (2000) report a survey of the literature by Froyd and Lambert (1989) which found 1,430 available measures.

In choosing a measure suitable for a group the facilitator should ensure that:

1   it is valid: it measures the change you want. It is pointless using a measure that doesn't pick up on the symptoms, distress and problems clients have as then it will be impossible for it to report changes and improvements;
2   it is feasible to use: it is easy for clients to fill in, easy to score, cheap to purchase, and broadly applicable to all the clients in your group;
3   it is reliable: generally its results are consistent and not subject to spurious change.

There are many measures to choose from on the market but two broadly applicable ones which are worth considering are the CORE (Clinical Outcomes in Routine Evaluation) outcome measure (Barkham et al., 1998; Core System Group, 1998) and the Outcome Questionnaire (OQ-45) (Lambert et al., 1996). The OQ-45 is a forty-five item questionnaire which provides comparable scores of the client's level of symptomatic distress, social and interpersonal functioning. The CORE has thirty-four items which provide ratings of client well-being, symptoms, life functioning and risk behaviours.

For those interested in measures targeted at specialist populations there are measures such as the Strengths and Difficulties Questionnaire (Goodman, 1997) which measures children's behavioural and emotional problems, or the Beck Depression Inventory (Beck, Steer & Garbin, 1988) which measures depression symptoms.

From a solution-focused perspective there has been an interest in developing measures which are positively formulated, thus measuring the emergence of solution thoughts and behaviours rather than simply the reduction of problems and symptoms. For example, Yvonne Dolan (1991) has developed the Solution-Focused Recovery Scale for survivors of sexual abuse and Ron Kral (1988) has developed the Solution Identification Scale for working with children and parents. In addition, many researchers outside the solution-focused therapy field have developed measures that highlight positive as well as negative behaviours, such as the Strengths and Difficulties Questionnaire (Goodman, 1997), reflecting a growing interest in strengths-based measures.

Measuring process
As well as measuring outcome and change, Duncan and Miller (2000) also recommend that the therapist gains feedback from clients about the process of the therapy to ensure that from their perspective they are experiencing a quality service and that the conditions for effective therapy are established. Before suggesting specific measures let us first consider what research studies reveal are the conditions for effective therapeutic change.

WHAT ARE THE CONDITIONS FOR THERAPEUTIC CHANGE?   In a widely cited survey of psychotherapy outcome studies, researchers concluded that there were four main process factors responsible for positive change which were common across all therapeutic models and disciplines (Assay & Lambert, 1999; Lambert, 1992). They also estimated the relative contribution of these factors to positive change as follows:

1   Client factors – client and environment strengths and resources (40 per cent).
2   Quality of therapeutic relationship or alliance (30 per cent).
3   Expectancy, hope and placebo factors (15 per cent).
4   Therapeutic model and technique (15 per cent).

What is striking about these results is the high importance of client factors in an effective therapy. A quality therapeutic process recognises clients' central role in change and invites their active participation in therapy, involving their resources, strengths and ideas. Yalom (1995) cites a number of groupwork studies which suggest that it is the more active and involved member who benefits most (for example, Lundgren & Miller, 1965). Other studies have shown that members who assume leadership and other active roles in the group show greater improvement and adjustment over time (for example, Rappaport et al., 1992).

Secondly, and perhaps less surprisingly, is the contribution of a good therapeutic alliance. The degree to which the client feels understood, respected by the therapist and that the two are working on the same goal establishes the conditions for a positive outcome. Research has repeatedly found that a positive therapeutic alliance is the single best predictor of positive outcome (Krupnick et al., 1996; Orlinsky, Grawe, & Park, 1994). Interestingly, many studies show that it is the client's perception of the alliance as opposed to that of the therapist that matters most (Bachelor, 1991; Gurman, 1977), justifying the need to gain systematic feedback from the client rather than relying on therapist judgement. In groupwork, the corresponding construct of 'group cohesiveness' – the degree to which members feel drawn to and accepted by the group – is also an essential precondition to the group functioning (Yalom, 1995). Though less well-researched than the alliance in individual therapy, Yalom (1995) cites a growing number of studies which indicate its centrality in outcome (Hurley, 1989; Yalom et al., 1967).

Thirdly, a quality therapeutic process instils a client's hope and optimism for change. Many studies have revealed that if clients can be encouraged to believe change is possible then this is a major contribution to a positive outcome (Snyder et al., 1999). Even in clinical studies in the treatment of depression researchers have found that an inert placebo can be as powerful as psychoactive drugs, when patient and/or doctor believe that it is going to work (Greenberg & Fisher, 1997).

Finally, the tasks and techniques of therapy also contribute to a quality process, though in a much more minor way than the contribution of client and relationship factors above. In fact, it is arguable that the therapeutic technique contributes the most when it activates the other factors above. For example, perhaps the greatest contribution of solution-focused therapy's techniques to outcome is the emphasis they place on utilising client strengths and resources, achieving a collaborative therapeutic relationship and instilling optimism and hope for change.

SESSION PROCESS RATING FORM   In order for a session process rating form to determine whether the group conditions for therapeutic change are established, it needs to gain client feedback about aspects of the group functioning highlighted above such as:

1   whether the client feels supported and understood within the group;
2   whether they feel involved and able to participate;
3   whether the goals, content and tasks of the group are helpful to them.

Indeed the act of seeking feedback from clients activates some of the conditions of a quality therapeutic process, in that it establishes the therapy as collaborative and values their input and ideas in shaping how it progresses. Duncan and Miller (2000) suggest a number of session rating forms for individual therapy such as the Session Rating Scale (Johnson, 1994) or the Working Alliance Inventory (Hovarth & Greenberg, 1989). Figure 6.1 shows a group session rating form, which can be specifically applied to groups.

In analysing the results of the group session rating form, it is important to bear in mind that in practice clients tend to under-report problems in this area (Miller, 1998). If a client is dissatisfied with therapy they tend to drop out rather than report to the therapist and will even say verbally that 'things are going OK' when in fact they have a number of dissatisfactions with the therapeutic process. For this reason therapists should assess any middle scores on the scale as indicating a problem. Thus a *score of three* on any of the questions can be taken as an indication of dissatisfaction and should be addressed by the therapist.

Carrying out ongoing group evaluation

In their model of 'client-directed, outcome-informed' individual therapy, Duncan and Miller (2000) recommend the following steps:

1   Client arrives five minutes early for the session and completes the outcome measure(s).
2   Therapist and client score the outcome measure(s) together and they use the results to inform the therapy. In the first session the measure highlights current issues and goals. In later sessions it highlights improvements and change. If there is no change as reported by the measures, this is used as a basis for a collaborative discussion about what could be done differently to promote change. It is hoped that the 'objective' measures will free up those clients who might under-report problems, to honestly discuss their progress.

We are interested in hearing your views and feedback about the group meeting today so as to help us keep on track and ensure the group meets your needs and goals. Please be frank and honest which will help us the most

Name: **Date:**

Please rate how much you agree or disagree with the following statements:

1)   I felt the group content today was relevant to my needs and goals.

    Disagree Strongly   *Agree Strongly*
       1   2   3   4   5

2)   I found the group today helpful to me achieving my goals.

    Disagree Strongly   *Agree Strongly*
       1   2   3   4   5

3)   I felt understood and supported in the group today.

    Disagree Strongly   *Agree Strongly*
       1   2   3   4   5

4)   I felt I had enough group time today.

    Disagree Strongly   *Agree Strongly*
       1   2   3   4   5

5)   I felt involved and active in the group today.

    Disagree Strongly   *Agree Strongly*
       1   2   3   4   5

6)   I felt hopeful about progress at the end of the meeting today.

    Disagree Strongly   *Agree Strongly*
       1   2   3   4   5

7)   I found the group tasks helpful and relevant today.

    Disagree Strongly   *Agree Strongly*
       1   2   3   4   5

8)   I felt the facilitator managed the group well today.

    Disagree Strongly   *Agree Strongly*
       1   2   3   4   5

Anything particularly helpful today that you would like <u>more</u> of?

Anything particularly unhelpful today that you would like <u>less</u> of?

Any other comments

Figure 6.1   *Group session rating form*

3   Near the end of the session, the therapist asks the client to complete the session rating form and then views this to see if it highlights any problems in the alliance or process of therapy. If the client scores a middle or low score on any of the questions, the therapist initiates a discussion about how the therapy is progressing and about how it could be improved, for example, 'what could happen in the session to move the score from a three to a four?'

Duncan and Miller (2000) recommend that the above sequence be carried out for each session that the client attends. Their rationale is that it is impossible to predict the length of treatment or at which session a client will drop out. In addition, if a process problem does emerge during a session, the session rating form allows for this to be picked up and addressed during that session, rather than the client leaving dissatisfied.

The conditions of groupwork are often quite different. Firstly, groups are usually contracted for a particular length of time, say, five to twelve sessions (though there is still the problem of early dropout). Secondly, in a group session there may not always be time to analyse each person's outcome measure at the beginning or their process measure at the end. Thirdly, group members often want an opportunity initially to discuss their dissatisfactions with progress on a one-to-one basis with the facilitator rather than with the group as a whole. For these reasons, I suggest a modified evaluation protocol for solution-focused groups below:

Protocol for groups

1   GOAL ATTAINMENT MEASURE   The initial goal form (see Figure 5.1) can be completed with the client during the pre-screening interview or during the first session. Given that creating well-formed, positive goals with clients can take some time, it can be productive to repeat this exercise at both the pre-screening interview and the first session in order to arrive at a positive, focused goal which the client is happy to work towards during the group. Progress towards goals can be reviewed at the beginning of each session using a review form (see Figure 5.2). Participants can complete the form individually and then share their progress with the group via a group round. The completion of the review form can become a starting ritual for the group, evoking the powerful and focusing scaling question: Since coming to the group please rate on a scale of one to ten where you are now with each of your goals? This can flow naturally into a

'review of progress' discussion (see Chapter 5), where changes and progress towards goals are elicited, amplified and reinforced. Blocks to progress can also be identified and addressed either in the group as a whole or in a separate individual meeting. During the last session an 'end of group' review form (see Figure 5.3) can be used to consolidate gains from the beginning to the end and to highlight any steps to be taken beyond the end of the group.

2   STANDARDISED PSYCHOMETRIC MEASURE   Though it is feasible to invite clients to complete the standardised measure at the beginning of each group session as recommended by Duncan and Miller (2000), in groupwork it may be practically difficult (given that in an average group eight or ten forms would have to be processed). It may be thus more practical to apply these measures at key points over the course of the group, for example:

1   At the pre-screening and follow-up interviews.
2   During the first and last sessions.
3   At pre-screening, mid-session review, and follow-up interview.

The first and third suggestions have the advantage of being conducted in an individual interview when there can be ample time to analyse and discuss the implications of the results with the client.

3   SESSION PROCESS RATING FORM   Clients should complete the session process rating form at the end of the session and it should take them no longer than one minute. They can be introduced as follows:

> Just before we finish, please take a moment to fill in the session rating forms, to give us an idea how you found tonight and whether you want anything different. Just leave them for me on your way out/to the tea room.

The therapists then analyse the forms during their post-break review and use the information to help them plan the next group session and to highlight any individual issues that need to be addressed with clients. If possible, it can be helpful for the therapists to be available to the clients for a few minutes after the group has ended giving space for clients to approach them about any 'leftover' issues from the group. This has the advantage of highlighting any problems and can avoid dropout. To invite clients to approach informally at the end of the meeting you can simply add the following sentence to the introduction above:

If anybody has anything they want to discuss about today's meeting, I will be available after the group for a few minutes. Please come up to me. Or, if you would prefer, please feel free to ring me during the week.

4   FOLLOWING UP ON FEEDBACK   Ongoing evaluation gives the facilitator an opportunity to address problems and issues early on and this can be done in a number of ways. Firstly, it can be addressed in the group as a whole. As we have discussed above, reviewing goals can be incorporated in the beginning of the session. When obstacles to change are identified, the group can be encouraged to work together supportively to find solutions and ways to overcome the impasse. When there are process issues as indicated by the session rating form, the facilitator can initiate a group discussion about the issue in question and attempt to reach a group consensus about the way forward, perhaps negotiating a new way of structuring the group.

Secondly, the facilitator can follow up on feedback by making use of the informal time in the group. The social or refreshment time during the group, the few minutes as people arrive and depart at the beginning and end of the group respectively all provide an opportunity for the facilitator to interact with group members seeking their views and opinions. For example, if the facilitator is concerned that one member is withdrawn he/she can use informal time to reach out and connect with this person and to draw them into conversation with others. Or if one member is having difficulty in the group the facilitator can use this time to offer support and even explore whether anything else can be done to help.

Thirdly, the facilitator can follow up by telephoning clients in between sessions. For example, if a session rating form indicates a problem the facilitator can simply ring the client in question saying they would like to discuss how the group is going and what could make it better. Therapists who are unsure about using such 'outreach' methods should consider the research evidence. Miller and Rollnick (1991) cite a number of studies that show a decline in dropout when therapists simply follow up first or missed attendances with a telephone call (Koumans, Muller & Miller, 1967; Nirenberg, Sobell & Sobell, 1980).

Fourthly, the facilitator can follow up by arranging an individual meeting with the client in addition to the group session. This can be a scheduled meeting as is the case with screening, mid-point reviews and post-group interviews or it can be done on an *ad hoc* basis following consideration of a client's progress according to their outcome and process measures. Though time-consuming, such meetings can be extremely valuable in ensuring clients' progress and the group's survival.

Ongoing evaluation in action

Case 1
Joe, a psychologist, was facilitating a six-week assertiveness and communication skills course which involved a great deal of skills practice and role-play which Joe saw as essential to learning and therapeutic change. By session two, two people had not returned and the session rating forms indicated some problems. Many people reported that they found the role-plays 'uncomfortable and embarrassing'. Joe rang the members who missed the meeting and they gave similar feedback. At session three, Joe apologised for not 'getting it right' and opened a discussion on 'what way the group should be run'. After much debate the group agreed that they would like a primarily discussion-based group with only some role-play for those who found it helpful. After this revision the group became cohesive and completed successfully.

Case 2
Mary, a single parent of four children, was referred by a child protection agency to an eight-week parenting group to help her manage her oldest son's difficult behaviour. By session four, though Mary reported on the session rating form that she felt understood and supported in the group, it was clear from the outcome measures that things were in fact worse with her son and his behaviour had escalated out of control. The therapist arranged a review meeting with Mary who revealed that she was depressed and under a huge amount of pressure from her ex-partner and that getting to the group was a problem for her. They agreed that something different needed to be done. They arranged an emergency case conference with the child protection agency and extra family supports were put in place. It was arranged for her son to be placed with a foster family four days a week. Given the extra support Mary was able to attend the rest of the group. By the end, the measures showed that though the group had been supportive outside events had taken over and stopped her from fully participating. As a result she had not made the gains she would have wished in terms of her parenting. With the agreement of the therapist, she re-attended the group the following term, when things were settled. In the second group she made better gains as reported by outcome measures and she made a better contribution to the group taking on a supportive role to other parents.

Case 3
Alec was attending a five-week social skills group at his mental heath day centre. By session two, he was not progressing on his outcome

measures and his session rating scores were low. The therapist arranged to meet Alec, who revealed that he felt an outsider in the group. He was from a different culture and background than all the others and he felt they looked down on him. This was news to the therapist who had been 'blind' to Alec's cultural differences. In discussing how to proceed Alec said that he did not want to raise the issues in the group given how short it was, so they looked at what other community resources he might attend and the possibility of establishing a group culturally matched to his needs at the centre. The therapist thanked Alec for 'opening his eyes' to the cultural issues he had not noticed before.

Alec did in fact attend the remaining sessions in the group and became more involved, to the extent that he did discuss in the last session how 'culturally different' he felt in the group. This contribution was valued by the other group members.

Summary

In this chapter we have described a method of ongoing evaluation that group therapists can incorporate into their work. The power of this ongoing evaluation is threefold. First, by its very nature it is collaborative and invites clients to be partners in the therapeutic process. Second, by being focused on change and goals it helps the therapy to be focused and brief, targeted on the goals and well-being of the client. Third, it allows for problems and difficulties to be highlighted early and enables the therapist to take action to review progress collaboratively with clients who are struggling and to 'do something different'. In this way therapeutic failure and drop-out can be avoided and, if the therapy is ultimately going to be unsuccessful, this can be highlighted early and alternative arrangements considered.

7
Managing 'Difficult' Groups

The Buddha was meditating beneath the Bodhi tree, waiting for enlightenment. Mara, unhappy with the Buddha's peacefulness, sent his army to destroy him. The army approached with rocks, clubs and arrows to discharge at the Buddha. But he remained unperturbed, sitting peacefully and meditating, surrounded by a golden aura of light. Enraged, Mara ordered his army to unleash their missiles to destroy the Buddha. However, when the missiles entered the Buddha's aura, they were immediately transformed into flowers, which fell by his feet as if they were gifts to him.

Sangharakshita (1996)

Difficult situations regularly occur in groupwork and can present a great challenge to the facilitator. These situations can include members being excessively negative, directly confronting the facilitator, disrupting the group by erratic behaviour or monopolising group time. Difficulty is part and parcel of the ebb and flow of group process. Tuckman (1965) in his well-known 'forming, storming, norming, performing' metaphor for group development conceives the conflictual storming process as central to the formation of group identity. Despite the normality of these situations, they can be difficult to manage and require a skilled, thoughtful approach. This chapter looks at a solution-focused approach to the difficult situations that occur in groupwork. By thinking more constructively and taking into account clients' level of motivation, facilitators can respond differently to overcome group impasses and client 'resistance'. The ideas are illustrated by case examples and a generic supervision exercise (see Figure 7.1) to help therapists generate constructive descriptions and ways forward with difficult cases.

Complainant level of motivation

In Chapter 4 we described the different levels of motivation, notably visitor, complainant and customer, at which clients could be at with respect to certain therapeutic goals and group contexts. Clients at the customer level of motivation are ideal, they have clear goals and are motivated to work towards them. Clients at the more common visitor and complainant levels of motivation are at an earlier stage of the change process and are often experienced as 'difficult' by facilitators and therapists. Visitors are experienced as difficult because of their lack of engagement in the group or their refusal to attend in the first place. Complainants are experienced as difficult because they make extra demands on the facilitator, are often in conflict with them and seem to make apparently little progress towards their goals. In Chapter 4 we have already described different ways of engaging clients at the visitor level of motivation. In this chapter we look at the particular challenges posed by complainants, considering what facilitators can do differently to engage complainants. As Miller and Rollnick (1991: 100) state:

> Dramatic differences in client resistance have been shown when the *same* therapists take different approaches with clients (Miller & Rollnick, 1991), or even switch styles within the same session (Patterson & Forgatch, 1985).

Clients at the complainant level of motivation have a goal and often desire it greatly but they feel powerless to effect change and to move towards it. They are either hopeless about the possibility of change, such as a relapsed drug user who has given up on ever quitting, or they are angry and dissatisfied with professional services such as the veteran mental health user who believes the 'system' has not helped with his or her difficulties and has made things actually worse. Generally, goals at the complainant level of motivation are negatively formulated, such as 'giving up drugs' or 'not being depressed'. The therapeutic alliance is often poor, clients believe that the therapist is not actually helping or may even be hindering them in the pursuit of their goals.

From a solution-focused perspective, complainants need a different approach in order to renegotiate a 'customer contract' with them. The aim is to discover goals which tap into their great motivation, highlight examples of how they can effect change in their lives and to transform the therapeutic alliance from a conflictual to a co-operative basis. Though dealing with complainants can be demanding for a facilitator it can also become a pivotal point in the development of the group. Clients at the complainant level of motivation often have great energy and drive for change, and once a co-operative rather than a conflictual alliance is formed this can become a great resource and inspiration for the group. In short, clients who were 'thorns in the side' of facilitators for part of the group can become their greatest allies once the facilitators find ways of co-operating with them.

Co-operating with complainants

- Think differently/seek constructive understanding.
- Provide nurture and support.
- Go at the client/group's pace.
- Review progress with the group/client.
- Therapist self-care.

Box 7.1 *Co-operating with complainants*

Think differently/seek constructive understanding

> The most difficult people in our lives are our greatest teachers if
> we can be wise enough to learn from them. Rather than resenting
> their presence, we should welcome them and eagerly look forward
> to what wisdom they will offer us.
>
> Author's own

Traditionally 'resistance' or 'difficulty' was thought of as residing
within the individual. Clients were perceived as being the source of
the problems that occurred in group process. While also critiquing
the value of pathological labels elsewhere in the book, Yalom (1995)
in his classic *The Theory and Practice of Group Psychotherapy* dedi-
cates a chapter to describing the various types of 'problem patients'
that present in groups and whose personality type contributes to
stuckness or problematic group process. From a solution-focused
perspective, resistance is not perceived as residing in the pathology of
the individual but as something relational and contextual. The fact
that a group gets bogged down and stuck is a function of poorly
constructed therapeutic goals and methods and in particular a poor
therapeutic alliance. If facilitators think negatively or pathologically
about the clients in the group this can be indirectly communicated as
criticism and can compromise the therapeutic alliance, thus creating
resistance. Consider the following case example 7.1:

Case Example 7.1 Group members confront the facilitator

This is a heterogeneous group of seven members with the common goal
of achieving better interpersonal relationships. The facilitator experiences the group as 'avoidant' and 'shallow'. He feels that they only
remain on the level of social chitchat, and avoid issues of depth. In
session three, one of the group members, Anna, makes a disclosure
about how she felt abandoned as a child by her mother's death.
Immediately, another member, Robert, changes the subject of conversation to something else. The other group members go with Robert's

flow. The facilitator is annoyed that Anna's point is lost. He interrupts the conversation saying: 'Anna just said something important, yet it wasn't listened to in the group.' There is a silence. The therapist waits, and then asks Anna if she wants to say something. She shakes her head and there is a return to silence. The facilitator offers the suggestion that perhaps the group feels more comfortable with social chitchat rather than real conversation, but that he wonders if this is really the purpose of the group. There is further silence, and then Robert speaks up, criticising the facilitator, asking what does he know about the purpose of the group. Other members join in, criticising the facilitator on his handling of the group.

In Case Example 7.1 the facilitator held a critical understanding of how the group was functioning (i.e. the members being shallow and avoidant). This understanding crept into his 'scolding' of the group for not listening and for being more comfortable with social chitchat rather than 'real' conversation. It is likely that his tone of voice in offering these understandings revealed his frustration and annoyance. It is therefore not surprising that the group responded in the 'avoidant way' they did (thus reinforcing the facilitator's judgement of them). From a solution-focused perspective the aim is for the therapist to think differently and to seek a constructive understanding of the clients and the group's behaviour. In Case Example 7.1, the facilitator could have conceived of the group's ability to relate socially as a possible strength and understand their wish not to discuss more difficult issues as a possible expression of concern – that they don't want to upset one another. The facilitator could have reviewed progress with the group and checked out if the method (chitchat) was helping them progress towards their goals. Holding a constructive understanding is likely to make this conversation less confrontative and more co-operative.

If as a therapist, you find yourself tempted to react negatively to clients' narrative or to disagree with them, or if you feel that you 'just can't understand why they are behaving they way they do', or if you feel defensive or frustrated by clients' responses, then a good working assumption is that you are not thinking constructively about these clients – you have not appreciated or understood their perspective sufficiently. Such thinking is likely to be communicated indirectly to clients and to increase the difficulty further. It can be best in these situations to step back and try to reassess what the client is saying and then to come up with new constructive frames. Case Examples 7.2 and 7.3 consider how facilitators can think more constructively about challenges from clients in groups and the numerous constructive responses and questions that can flow from this understanding.

Case Example 7.2   'I don't know what this group can do for me'

Luke is forty-six years old and a veteran of the mental health services who has received many different diagnoses. He has attended many different groups and services and has a reputation for being difficult. He is now starting a group in the mental health day centre focused on teaching 'daily coping skills'. When during an initial group round he is asked to state his goals for the group, he states:

'To be honest, I don't know what this group can do for me. I've being coming to this clinic and other mental health services for twenty-four years now and I wonder if things are actually worse. I'm not sure of any groups that have been helpful. No offence, but they have all been pretty useless.'

(Though in reality these issues might have been best addressed in a screening interview, it often happens in a busy practice that such interviews don't get done and the therapist is faced by such an initial challenge.)

Constructive understanding

Luke really wants things to be different but is frustrated at not knowing how to go about achieving this. Correctly, he realises that the services are not the key to him making progress but rather his own efforts and resources.

He is articulate and assertive and wants to make sure he gets the best service. He learns by challenging and criticising ideas. He also has extensive experience and knowledge of mental heath services from a customer point of view. By virtue of the fact he is continuing to attend he is committed to getting something from them. He could be a real resource to the group.

Possible constructive responses

Reframe: strength   You have attended many courses in the past, you really have put in a lot of effort and commitment into trying to solve your problems . . . what does it say about you that you have responded with such commitment?

Exception   Of all the things you have tried, which have made things a little bit better? Which have worked even if it is only slightly?

Reframe: resource   Given your experience of the mental health services, and the different groups you have attended, what way do you think groups should be run? What should be borne in mind as we proceed in this group?

Coping   What I am interested in is how you cope with the situation – how you have managed up until now.

Acknowledging motivation   Sounds like you really want things to be different. What makes you want change that much? What difference would it make to you?

Establishing a goal   What I'm impressed with is your commitment. You don't have to attend this group, yet you've come clearly hoping to gain something. What brings you back? What keeps you coming?

Minimal goal setting   I'm aware that meeting over a few weeks won't produce a miracle, but suppose it could help in a small way, what would you like to see happening over the next few weeks? What small change would you like to see?

Case Example 7.3   Monopolising group time

In a heterogeneous group one of the clients, Jean seems to talk more than most. She is the first to speak in group discussions and seems to interrupt other people when they are talking. The facilitator is concerned that this is disrupting the group and that Jean is beginning to get on everyone's nerves.

Constructive understanding

People who talk a lot in groups are usually very motivated to participate, and to contribute their ideas and experience. They generally will take on responsibility in the group for tasks, etc. and can be an asset in this way. They are often unaware of how much time they take up and think they speak the same amount as everyone else. Inadvertently, facilitators often collude with an 'over-talkative' person by providing too much attention (for example, by looking at them to come in, or providing too much attention when they speak, or simply by the seating structure, for instance if Jean is in a prominent seat opposite the facilitator).

Possible responses

Attention

The facilitator should ensure that he/she is providing equal attention time to all clients by looking to quieter clients to come in or addressing questions directly to them, not giving attention to Jean every time she speaks and/or changing the seating structure in the room to provide better distribution of space. How a facilitator uses their body language can be very powerful in shaping group process.

Structure

The facilitator can introduce a timed group round or exercises whereby people are allocated a certain amount of time to speak and one member of the group (this could be Jean) is selected to manage this.

Polite interrupting

> *Therapist*: [*addressing whole group when Jean answers first*] Don't leave it to Jean all the time to answer for the group, let's hear from some other people . . .

Giving responsibility

By meeting Jean individually the therapist can discuss Jean's progress and raise the need in the group to ensure that everyone speaks. The therapist could seek Jean's help in drawing out the quieter members. Jean could also be a resource to the group in 'taking on' challenging role-plays or other structured exercises which other members might be reluctant to do at first.

Review in group

If there is sufficient trust in the group, it may be possible to encourage the group to provide constructive feedback to Jean which includes their valuing her willingness to contribute as well as their wish for a more balanced use of time (which other group members and the facilitator are equally responsible for).

Provide nurture and support

Complainants often feel hopeless and despairing about their situation. They have a goal that they feel powerless to work towards. Many of their feelings are akin to being 'burnt out' and battle weary. Many therapists mistakenly look, too early on, for these clients to assume responsibility and to do something different about the problem that is afflicting them. However, clients at the complainant level of motivation are not ready to do anything, they need to be *first nurtured, supported and understood*. Facilitators do best by adopting a sympathetic and supportive attitude towards these clients, giving them time and space, and for this to be done without excessively focusing on the negatives of their situation.

> Client: It's pretty useless. I'm never going to overcome my depression.
> Therapist: I'm sorry you feel that way. You've had a really rotten week, haven't you? With that row with your boss which really unsettled and undermined you. It's understandable that you are feeling low. I'm sure other people in the group have felt the same way when they've had a setback [*therapist draws on group support*] . . . You need to make sure you're looking after yourself next week.

In a solution-focused group, there may not be sufficient group time to support a person who is struggling with a problem, but these clients can also be supported outside the group time. It can be very powerful for the facilitator to make a special point to talk to these people during the tea and coffee time after the group, or to ring them between groups to see how they are doing, or even to offer a separate individual meeting aside from the group. This can be experienced by the client as a demonstrable show of support and it avoids too much of the group time being taken up with problem talk. Other nurturing gestures can make a big difference. For example, the therapist making sure to make tea for the client at the end of the group with the comment: 'Look, you've had a difficult week, let me get you a cup of tea', can help the client feel cared for and supported. The essential point is that the provision of social support either within the group or outside it can help re-energise and re-motivate a client. It can also transform the therapeutic alliance into a constructive and co-operative relationship. Not surprisingly, in recalling the moments of therapy that made the greatest difference to them, clients rarely report the skilled interventions or questions of the therapists, but rather how in a human way they felt cared for and supported (Yalom, 1999)

When clients have had difficult weeks or are stuck negatively in a situation the suggestion of self-care or self-nurture exercises can be helpful in moving things forward.

> *Therapist*: You've been trying for many years to get your partner to stop drinking. Despite the way he has treated you, you have continued to care for him and continued to express ongoing care and love for him. [*Pause*] I'm wondering whether you could turn some of the care and love towards yourself and to do something next week for yourself that you might really enjoy or that you will find really relaxing. I think you really deserve it.

Go at the client's/group's pace

Brief therapy moves slowly.

Lipchik (1994)

One of the errors novice solution-focused therapists make is to move too quickly for the client. Misunderstanding the co-operative spirit of brief therapy they feel a sense of urgency and 'rush' to solution talk ahead of the client who is not ready to consider such an angle on their problems. This 'rush to be brief' (Lipchik, 1994) can spark off resistance in the client and leave them feeling misunderstood and not listened to. Therapists do well to take their clients' problems seriously and to listen carefully to their perspective. Clients will generally only take the therapist's lead to solution talk when they feel sufficiently understood and respected and that the therapist has a unique understanding of their life story rather than a general understanding of their problems. When a client or group appears stuck in their problem, it could well be that the therapist has 'gone ahead' of them. The therapist in this instance should step back, slow down, listen and attempt to constructively understand the client's position. Going slow means not necessarily having a solution or a way forward at the end of each session. It can be sufficient for the client to have some new ideas or questions to consider or simply to leave the group feeling supported and that the therapist and group members stand with him/her against the problem.

During group sessions, 'going at the client's pace' often requires a return to problem talk for a brief period. Reflective listening and drawing in other group members to support can be the best way for therapists to emphasise to the client that they have indeed understood the client's predicament and the seriousness of the problem. Consider the following example taken from the goal setting round in the first session of a group for parenting children with autism and other learning difficulties.

> *Facilitator*: What would you like to achieve by coming to this group?
>
> *Alice*: [*angry*] To be honest, I'm not sure if it can help at all. I first brought my child to this clinic when he started biting other children at the age of three. He's now eleven and I think he is actually worse.
>
> *Facilitator*: I'm sorry to hear that. [*Pause*] It must be really frustrating to be attending a clinic for so long concerned about your little boy, hoping that they can help you and then to feel they haven't helped at all. I can imagine that that must be really annoying.
>
> *Alice*: Tell me about it. Sometimes I feel really alone, that there is no one out there.
>
> *Facilitator*: Like there is no one to support you.
>
> *Alice*: Yeah, that it's just me and him.
>
> *Facilitator*: That must feel pretty lonely at times.
>
> *Alice*: Yeah.
>
> *Facilitator*: And I'm sure other people in the group have had similar experiences, of being frustrated by the lack of help from services and dealing with things on their own.
>
> *Ian*: Absolutely, when my wife left me because of my child's problems, I felt totally abandoned and blamed . . .
>
> [*Many clients in the group come in at this stage relaying similar experiences and there is a great deal of group support.*]

Coping questions can also be useful for clients who seem stuck in their problem narrative and who do not appear ready to move to solution talk. The function of these questions is to help uncover with the clients the story of how they are coping on a daily basis with the problem that affects them. The aim is not to challenge their beliefs or ask them to think or do things differently. Rather the aim is to give voice to their struggles and resistance to the influence of the problem and to uncover the strengths and resources they have in spite of its effects. Such conversations with clients can be very empowering and can result in an improved therapeutic alliance indirectly identifying the therapist as an ally to the client in their fight against the problem. These ideas have resonance with Alan Wade's (1997) approach of identifying the client's 'acts of resistance' and the narrative therapy concepts of 'externalising the problem' (White & Epston, 1990). Consider the above example continued:

> *Facilitator*: So you have been saying how in dealing with your child's problems that the services haven't helped as much as you would have liked (and I agree with you that they are pretty limited and it is not good enough) and that you have felt pretty much on your own . . . What I am interested in knowing is how you have managed this. Given the significant difficulties your child has, how have you coped? What has made a difference?
>
> *Alice*: I don't know . . .
>
> *Facilitator*: Well, it strikes me that you have managed to achieve a lot, for example getting him settled in school, in spite of these difficulties. I'm curious how you did this.
>
> *Alice*: Well, I guess it's important to keep fighting. You can't let the services off the hook. You have to be really assertive to make sure they give you what your child needs.
>
> *Facilitator*: Ah, I see.
>
> *Ian*: That's what I have found too. They will try and fob you off but you have to come back to them.
>
> *Therapist*: I see, so as a group you have to be persistent to ensure the services don't fob you off.

Often when the problems have been taken seriously and the coping responses validated, clients who were originally in conflict with the purposes of the group can begin to consider making goals. Though these may initially be minimal, they can be a catalyst for the creation of powerful collective goals, which can drive the group forward.

> *Facilitator*: Given what you are saying, what can we achieve in this group that would be helpful to you?
>
> *Alice*: I guess I want to feel energised again. I've been feeling pretty low recently. I'd like to have more energy to take up the fight again.
>
> *Facilitator*: You want to feel re-energised. I think the group can help you with that. [*Looks to other group members.*]
>
> *Ian*: Yeah, we need to stick together.
>
> *Susan*: Maybe we should take on the services together.
>
> *Alice*: How do you mean?

Susan: You know, campaign to get better facilities for the children.
Gina: Or maybe we could do things together and share things like
   babysitting . . .

The above example illustrates how challenges or difficult situations
in groupwork can be opportunities for the facilitator. Handled well,
such situations can act as catalysts for deepening trust between group
members, increasing group cohesion and transforming the alliance
between the therapist and the whole group. So often the client who is
initially the 'most difficult' can, when the context changes, become
one of the most positively influential people in the group. Therapists
should remember that the client who is initially the greatest 'thorn in
their side' in the group, can often teach them something important
and in doing so can become their greatest ally.

Review progress with the group client
A common pathway to therapeutic stuckness occurs when the
therapist, in the face of the therapy failing, continues to 'do more of
the same' intervention in the hope that this will yield a different
result. For example, though historically a mental health client has
not benefited from a particular type of therapy, he may continue to
be offered it, in the belief that persistence will eventually pay off. Or
when medication prescribed for depression is not working, a patient
may be offered increased levels of the drug rather than an alternative
form of treatment. A central rule in solution-focused therapy that
aims to break this cycle of stuckness is simply: if it doesn't work,
don't do it again, do something different (Berg & Miller, 1992).
Arguably the rule applies to the solution-focused therapy model
itself. For some clients, a focus on goals, strengths and possibilities is
not what they are looking for. The may want a more Rogerian
approach, or even a past-focused psychodynamic approach. A good
solution-focused therapist should be flexible enough to adapt to the
client's wishes and unique way of co-operating even if it means
abandoning the solution-focused model if that is what is required.
   In a group context the therapist should endeavour to seek constant
feedback about whether progress is being made and about what is
and isn't working in the group process. As discussed in Chapter 6
this can be done by seeking feedback using evaluation and goal
review forms and then using these as a basis for discussing progress
either by meeting group members individually or in the group as
a whole. When difficulties emerge in a group the therapist has a
responsibility to take action to alter the course of the group treatment. If a group member is consistently struggling in the group, or is
being disruptive to other members, a useful way to proceed is to

arrange an individual meeting to review progress. The style of this meeting is not one of confrontation where the client is blamed for the difficulties, but one where the therapist seeks feedback from the client about the current impasse and about possibilities for moving forward:

> *Therapist*: I wanted to meet with you to hear how things are progressing for you, to understand whether you are on track to achieve your goals for the group, or whether we need to do anything different to help you get there.

Despite our best intentions there are many clients whom we cannot help as therapists or for whom groupwork is a negative or an unhelpful experience. This is not to say that these clients can never be helped but rather that this particular intervention with this particular therapist at this particular time has not helped. We have a responsibility in these instances to identify early on when cases are not progressing and to review with the client other options or possibilities in a non-blaming way. Selekman (1997) describes the technique of 'firing the therapist' whereby the therapist admits that he/she has 'obviously missed the boat in terms of understanding and helping them resolve their problems' (1997: 190) and offers them the services of another therapist. Typically, Selekman finds, this intervention can become a catalyst for change with the clients forming a more realistic and co-operative alliance with the original therapist.

However, in situations of serious difficulty, the therapist should not be afraid to consider ending a client's involvement in a group if they are clearly not making progress or their presence is being too disruptive to other members in the group. Once again this should be done as constructively as possible. There is no need to 'further pathologise' the client by blaming them for the problems. Rather it is more helpful for the therapist to take some responsibility for not creating a group which matched their needs in the first place. Consider the following example:

> Cloe a thirty-six year-old mental patient who became so distressed at the last group meeting that she attempted to self-harm during the session when anxiety overtook her. This caused great distress to all the group members. As a result the therapist decided to meet with Cloe to review progress.

> *Therapist*: I was sorry about what happened in the last session.
> *Cloe*: So was I.
> *Therapist*: It must have been very distressing for you, to have caused you to act like that.
> *Cloe*: It was very upsetting. I felt the whole group were picking on me.

Therapist: I'm sorry to hear that. We certainly don't want the group experience to make you so anxious like that. What could we do differently to make it feel safe for you?

Cloe: I don't know . . .

Therapist: The group doesn't seem the right place for you at the moment. Let's agree to take a break from the group meetings until we can figure out how the group can be safe and helpful for you and all the others there. Would you like to meet with me a few times to figure this out or whether something else would be better for you?

Cloe: OK.

Asking a client to leave a group should be done in a way that does not increase the pathological self-descriptions of the client or damage their access to other therapeutic options in the future. Rather it should be done in a way that is constructive and respectful and opens up future possibilities.

Therapist self-care

Though the ideas of solution-focused therapy are simple in principle, they can be difficult to apply in practice. To be constantly constructive, optimistic and respectful requires great energy and flexibility on the part of the therapist. Encountering difficult situations can cause this to wane. We can easily be overcome by negative feelings for our clients and feel hopeless about the possibility of progress. Certain clients and certain situations can stir up 'our own stuff' and we can be taken over by negative emotion and memories that make us less effective. Just as it is easy for clients to slip into complainant or visitor levels of motivation about their goals, so therapists can slip into visitor or complainant levels of motivation towards their own therapeutic work. For example, therapists become visitors when they feel detached or uninterested in their work or clients and they become complainants when they feel pessimistic about change and hopeless about being effective. If this happens therapists will not have the optimism and energy to take on difficult cases.

Collectively as a profession, certain 'types' of cases can cause us to become pessimistic and anticipate poor outcome. Just mention to most therapists that they are due to facilitate a group for 'borderline' or 'sociopathic' clients and it is likely to arouse apprehension and pessimism. Duncan, Hubble and Miller (1997) describe the 'four horsemen of impossibility', notably 'anxiety, urgency, pessimism and over-responsibility' which can overtake a therapist and compromise their ability to be effective. As the authors comment, 'these states, moods, or expectations contribute to the prediction or anticipation of impossibility' (1997: 38).

Often in difficult situations the temptation is to give into frustration, confrontation, one-upmanship and pathological thinking which can further create and reinforce the original difficulty. When frustrated by a case therapists will often resort to using 'negative labels' to describe the client's behaviour rather than looking at their own responsibility. As Duncan, Hubble and Miller (1997) state:

> Using the example of classical psychoanalysis, if the therapy totters, then there would be the temptation to see the client as more damaged than originally thought. It is not that the method does not fit; the analysand's personality may be too primitive to weather the frustration inherent in the psychoanalytic situation . . . Not surprisingly, in years past, if a psychoanalysis was failing, the 'patient' would begin to be seen as 'latent schizophrenic'. (1997: 44)

It is thus crucial for therapists to take steps to monitor and maintain their own mental health and resourcefulness. Therapists need to be self-aware enough to notice when negative emotions are prominent in their mind and take steps to ensure these don't become overwhelming. It can be helpful for them to understand the sources of these emotions if aroused by their own autobiography and ensure that these don't leak into the therapy. Supervision and consultation with colleagues is critical in this respect. One of the great advantages of co-facilitated groupwork is the access to the support and understanding of a co-facilitator. When in 'difficulty' a facilitator can rely on their colleague to support them or respond with a constructive group intervention. In addition, during a group break or a post-break review there is an opportunity to review and reflect upon what has occurred and to seek new constructive understandings and ways forward.

Therapists should do whatever is necessary so that they can approach each new situation with a 'beginner's mind', uncluttered by negative attributions and expectations. Even in the most difficult situations, the therapist should thwart the 'four horsemen of impossibility' and 'go slow', remaining open and respectful, constructive and optimistic, focused on possibilities and not over-responsible for outcome. In a nutshell therapists should cultivate Rogers' core therapeutic attitudes of genuineness, unconditional positive regard and empathic understanding towards the client (Rogers, 1986) even when faced with the most difficult situations. To do this they need to monitor and maintain their own mental health. If as a therapist you feel yourself becoming negative or embroiled in difficulty then it is important to pause, take time to reflect and to highlight your own self-care. If you find yourself slipping to the complainant level of motivation towards your own work, then apply the principles outlined in

Purpose

The purpose of this supervision exercise is to generate ideas as to how you might move forward with a 'difficult' client or situation within a group. The aim is to try to help you think differently about the situation by discovering new strengths and possibilities both within the group/client's resources and within your own approach to the group/client (and/or that of the professional agency).

The exercise can be done in pairs or in small groups, with one person nominated as speaker (the person with the 'difficult case'), another as interviewer and the rest as observers. The exercise can last between five and twenty minutes and can be repeated, alternating the roles. The exercise can be used as the basis of a supervision or consultation group.

Interview

The speaker identifies a piece of work with which he/she feels stuck or with which he/she would like consultation, and briefly describes the case background, the problems and his/her involvement. The interviewer listens constructively and guides the speaker to think differently about the case using the suggested questions below:

Thinking constructively about group/client

- What group/client strength does the impasse reveal?
- Despite the stuckness, what is going well for this group/client?
- What might their goals be?
- What are they doing constructively in spite of any difficulties?
- What do you like and admire about this client?
- What resources and strengths do they have access or potential access to?
- Who are the supporters/helpers of the group/client not considered previously?

Thinking differently about your practice

- What are you aiming for in the work that your group/client is not aiming for?
- What goals/methods of work do you agree upon with the group/client?
- What is going well in your work with this client (or in their contact with professional services)?
- What are you doing constructively as a therapist in spite of the difficulties/current impasse?
- What resources and strengths have you got as a therapist that might be a help to this group/client?

At the end of the exercise, the listener provides constructive feedback as do the observers (identifying any further worker/client strengths and possibilities for going forward that they have observed).

The speaker then evaluates any suggestions/points raised and decides which ideas they will take forward.

Figure 7.1   *Supervision exercise – with a 'difficult' case*

the chapter above towards yourself. Make sure you are nurtured and supported; seek constructive understanding; reconnect to your goals for your therapeutic work; and remember your basic values of being respectful and constructive. Figure 7.1 outlines a generic supervision exercise that you can use either by yourself or with another therapist to help generate ways forward when you are faced by a 'difficult case' in groupwork.

Summary

Difficult or challenging situations are part and parcel of groupwork and in fact can represent an opportunity for the facilitator to help the group move to a deeper level of cohesion and thus a more effective way of working. However, difficult situations are precisely that – difficult (and can spell a death knell for the group if they are not correctly managed). In this chapter I have argued that many of the problems associated with 'difficulty' can be transformed when therapists think differently and more constructively about what is happening in the group process. I have suggested that much of the difficulty is created by treating clients who are at lower level of motivation (for example, complainant) as if they were at a higher level. By returning to basic principles of nurturing and supporting clients, seeking constructive understanding, slowing down and going at their pace, measuring and reviewing progress and therapist self-care, contracts with most clients and groups can be established which are helpful and facilitate change. The last principle of therapist self-care is perhaps the most important. The group therapist should take steps (for instance, by seeking support, consultation and supervision) to ensure they remain flexible, energetic and optimistic in the face of challenging situations. As Duncan, Hubble and Miller (1997) state: 'the strongest weapon in overcoming impossibility is the belief that it can be done. This belief or expectation for success . . . is manifested in our unswerving trust in clients and our unbridled faith in the therapeutic alliance' (1997: 49).

8

Creative Exercises to Enhance Group Process

Structured exercises and activities can be a useful addition to solution-focused groups in helping build rapport between group members, energising a flagging group process, interrupting problem talk and in mobilising the group's resources on creative solution building. They can be particularly useful in brief groupwork where the aim is to help focus group members on solution building quickly and effectively. As Yalom (1995: 447) states: 'In a brief therapy format, they [structured interventions] may be invaluable tools to focus the group on its task and to plunge the group more quickly into its task.'

However, it is important to recognise that structured exercises themselves are not central to effective groups, but rather the *constructive group process* they can bring about. Facilitators should be careful not to confuse the media with the message. The goal is to facilitate group members to interact in group-centred solution talk (see Chapter 3) and not the completion of a dramatic or flashy structured exercise. Indeed, structured exercises can be unhelpful in groups if they are not properly timed or negotiated or if they do not fit with the group culture and members feel uncomfortable carrying them out. A study of brief encounter groups showed that groups with a high dependence on structured exercises had fewer members who made significant positive gains and more members who made significant negative gains than those groups which relied more on group process for change (Lieberman et al., 1973). Thus facilitators should be judicious in their use of creative exercises and use them, ideally, when they flow naturally from group process or are generated by group members themselves.

This chapter illustrates five sample types of structured exercises which can be used in solution-focused groupwork. It is by no means an exhaustive list, there are as many types of creative exercises as there are creative individuals. They simply represent those exercises that the author has found most useful and versatile in his own facilitation of groupwork.

- Miracle question using creative visualisation.
- Group brainstorm of solutions.
- Role play/dramatic exercises.
- Solution pictures/mind mapping.
- Self-modelling using video.

Box 8.1   *Creative exercises to enhance group process*

Miracle question using creative visualisation

Creative visualisation can be a very helpful way of generating concrete detail about preferred futures and goals. It has been adapted by many practitioners as a structured exercise in groupwork (e.g. Houston, 1984). The miracle question in particular can be readily enhanced using a visualisation exercise as follows:

1   Participants are asked to close their eyes and encouraged to relax. By following a script or improvising, the facilitator can 'talk' the participants into a relaxed state, using a variety of suggestions which invite participants to focus on their breathing, or progressively relax the different muscles in the body, or visualise scenes such as walking by a beach or descending stairs, or a combination of all three. There are many suggested scripts available (e.g. Barber, 1977; Gawain, 1995).

2   When relaxed, participants are asked to imagine the miracle has happened and their problem has disappeared. They are asked to imagine in detail this new solution situation: 'Right, you are now waking up the morning after this miracle has taken place and the problem has completely gone. But because you don't know yet that the miracle has taken place, you are going to be surprised at all the differences and changes you notice . . . So what do you notice first? . . . What tells you the miracle has happened? . . . How do you feel different? . . . What do you notice that is different about other people? etc.

3   After the visualisation participants are encouraged to reflect on what they noticed and learnt and any new details they discovered about their preferred solutions. This can be discussed initially in pairs before participants discuss what happened in the whole group.

The group format of the miracle question can have advantages over its use with individual clients. Many of the solutions generated by the clients have common links, and this can be very reinforcing when shared in the whole group. In addition, hearing other people's miracles can be motivating and inspiring and encourage people to develop their own. The group format can also be problematic, however, as some people can be more self-conscious following a guided fantasy within a group setting and thus opt out of it.

Creative visualisation can also be used to carry out a 'rehearsal' of a desired solution at the end of a session. In this case clients are asked to imagine themselves going home and carrying out what they have learnt or achieving what they want to be different. In this way they are to imagine themselves carrying out the miracle at home. For example, if the particular session focused on assertiveness with one's manager, the clients may imagine themselves confidently and calmly being assertive with their boss. This exercise has the effect of making the desired goal more tangible and more likely to occur. Indeed, many groupworkers (e.g. Quinn & Quinn, 1995) recommend incorporating creative visualisation as a ritual to mark the end of each session. During the visualisation, participants can be encouraged to recall exceptional times (when things were going well), to revisit their goals or to visualise themselves carrying out plans they have generated in the group. The ritual can become an important part of the group, both in helping members slow down and experience the solutions they seek and in providing a relaxing, nurturing end to the group which in itself can be an 'exception' to the stressed lives that the clients lead.

Group brainstorm of solutions

Solution-focused groupwork not only helps clients generate their own solutions but also allows them to access the solutions of others, thus having the benefit of other people's knowledge as well as their own. A 'group brainstorm of solutions' can be a very useful group exercise to ensure that members have an opportunity to systematically contribute their solutions and ideas in response to a particular problem. The exercise can be planned in advance as a way of generating ideas and solutions to a specific issue. For example, in a group on anger management there may be a planned group brainstorm on 'what is the best way to calm down in a conflictual situation?' Or the brainstorm can be introduced on the spur of the moment during the group process, acting as a way of interrupting problem talk and moving the discussion on to the next stage. For example, if a client is describing a problem and the therapist is stuck in a problem-focused dialogue, a possible way of refocusing the group conversation is to introduce a brainstorm in the following way:

Therapist: That's a difficult problem you are dealing with. [*Therapist gets up and walks to the flip chart.*] Shall we get some ideas from the group in how they think you could move forward? Would you be interested in that?

Note in the above sequence the facilitator's body language of getting up and moving to the flip chart can have the effect of breaking a stuck, problem-focused dialogue. The physical action of group members turning to face the flip chart (meaning they are now facing the same way, working together) can pause and refocus a group discussion. Once the group brainstorming exercise has been introduced by the facilitator, it can be completed with the following four steps:

1   Client gives brief description of problem.
2   Goal setting.
3   Group brainstorm of potential solutions.
4   Client evaluates potential solutions.

The timing of a brainstorming exercise is crucial. If the client does not feel sufficiently supported then it may be too early to introduce such a collective solution-focus and it may be more appropriate to draw on group support by inviting other group members to share their experience of similar problems (see Chapter 3). A good rule of thumb about timing is as follows: when, as the facilitator, you feel tempted to offer solutions to a client, then this is a good time to pause and ask the group members to generate these ideas themselves. By doing this you activate the group therapeutic factors, build cohesion and help clients find more enduring solutions.

Consider Case Example 8.1 taken from a parenting group, which illustrates the four stages of a group brainstorm of solutions and some of the difficulties of getting the timing right.

Case Example 8.1   A group brainstorm of solutions in a parenting group

Stage 1   Brief description of problem

Andrea: My daughter, Joan, never goes to bed on time. Even when I get her to her room, she comes downstairs a few minutes later. And then I lose my head with her.

Therapist: That can be a difficult problem. I'm sure a lot of people in the group have experienced this. [*Lots of nods.*]

Andrea: I just don't know how to get her to bed.

Stage 2   Goal setting

Therapist: What way would you like things to go at bedtime?
Andrea: Well, I would like her to go to bed at a set time and then to stay in bed through the night. She is eight years old now, that is not too much to ask for.

Stage 3   Group brainstorm of potential solutions

Therapist: Would you be interested in hearing some ideas from the group about how they might try to get her to go to bed.
Andrea: Yeah.
Therapist: OK, we will go round the group and get as many ideas as possible, and I'll write them on the flip chart. You can decide at the end which ones you feel might work for you. OK? [*Nods*] Right let's start. How might Andrea get Joan to bed on time?
Peter: Well, you could try and give her a reward if she goes on time.
Andrea: That would never work with Joan. She never . . .
Therapist: Can I make a suggestion? [*Andrea nods.*] Let's get all the ideas on the flip chart first, and then you can decide at the end which ideas, if any, are helpful. Let the others in the group do a bit of hard work for a change! You sit back, listen and enjoy! OK.

Andrea smiles and agrees. The group then lists several useful ideas, such as establishing a good routine, working as a team with her partner, making sure Joan gets no attention when she's out of bed, being firm etc., which the therapist lists on the flip chart.

Stage 4   Client evaluates potential solutions

Therapist: OK, there is a big list of ideas. [*Therapist recaps the ideas.*] Right, [*addressing Andrea*] which ones do you think might work for you?
Andrea: Well, I think I have to be a bit firmer with her when she comes out of the room. I remember, when my husband is home and he supports me, and I'm firm I can get her to bed.
Therapist: Really. So that is something you have done already which has worked for you. Tell me more about how you managed to do it?

Case Example 8.1 illustrates how the brainstorming exercise can refocus a group on solution generation rather than problem description. Used successfully it can build cohesion and empower the group, giving members an opportunity to help one another, implicitly valuing their own knowledge. By the facilitator moving to list solutions on a flip chart and suggesting the participant sit back and listen, a problem interaction can be broken. The case example above also illustrates a danger of the exercise if used too early in a group before sufficient trust has been established. The parent initially interrupted the brainstorm of ideas, possibly because she felt they undermined her own skills as a parent. Notice how the facilitator used humour to reframe this process not as one of undermining but as one of nurturing. She was allowed to relax and listen as the group members gave her their best ideas. This allowed her to step back and gain a new perspective on the problem. By the end, the list of brainstormed ideas provoked her into remembering how she had been able to solve the problem in the past.

Role play/dramatic exercises

J.L. Moreno, the founder of psychodrama, and regarded by many as the father of group psychotherapy (Badaines, 1988), was the first to apply drama techniques to groupwork (Moreno, 1964). Many of these original ideas are relevant to a solution-focused approach to groupwork. By encouraging clients to 'act out' the miracle or pre-ferred solution, witnessed by the supportive audience of the group, solutions can become more concrete, realistic and better rehearsed. Though there are many variations, drama can be introduced as a way of moving from problem to solution talk with the following steps:

1   *Client is invited to take centre stage*
    In this format a client is invited to take centre stage in the group and to 'act out' the problem and solution in front of the group. Often, this is best done in an informal way, for example, a client who is describing a problem can be invited by the therapist: 'Can you show us what goes on at home, so we can all understand clearly?'
2   *Client acts out problem in drama*
    The client describes a 'core scene' in the problem and acts it out with the help of the group. For example, in a family dispute the client may select various members of the group to play his/her family members. With the help of the facilitator, the client then directs the scene and observes what happens.
3   *Exploration and change*
    The facilitator then invites a number of changes to the drama, the most important of these being role reversal (Badaines, 1988). If the client is standing outside the drama, he/she will be invited to change roles with one of the actors and to enter into the

drama, or if the client is playing him/herself, he/she will be invited to swap roles with a family member and to gain this perspective. The aim is to encourage the client to experience the problem from many different perspectives and also to move from being experientially involved (thus being able cathartically to express feelings) to being the director (thus gaining a reflective distance from the problem).

4   *Client acts out the solution*
The client is invited to describe the solution and how he/she would like it to be reversed. If needed the group can be invited to share ideas and brainstorm solutions. The client then gets the group to act out the solution and, with the coaching of the facilitator, takes on the different roles to ensure the solution is richly and fully described.

5   *Review*
A critical end to the exercise is the review. The client is encouraged to sum up the experience and to say which ideas he/she will be taking forward. Other group members are invited to comment, both by giving constructive feedback to the client and by identifying what they have personally learnt from the drama sequence. If the original scene is typical of the problems faced by other group members then this vicarious learning can be significant. In a brief group the facilitator should endeavour to pick a client whose problem (and solution) has resonance with as many other people in the group as possible.

Often role-play or drama is difficult to introduce in a group as the members or the facilitator(s) feel uncomfortable with it. As with all creative exercises, it is important not to impose them and to give members a choice about participating. Role-playing is not essential in groupwork by any means but can be very helpful in providing a novel way of breaking through problem talk. Drama can provide a good way of engaging clients at the complainant level of motivation who feel that the therapist or the group do not really appreciate the depth of their problem and who would welcome group time and attention to express this. For example, a client who continually describes relationship problems outside the group and for whom constructive questions by the facilitator have not created a shift can be invited: 'Can you show the group how the problem goes, so we can understand more clearly?'

Group participation in role-play is helped when the facilitator feels comfortable with role-play him/herself and is prepared to participate. Case Example 8.1 above could be enhanced by role-play in the following way:

Case Example 8.2   Drawing out solutions using role-play

This is a repeat of Case Example 8.1, where the solution-building process with the group is enhanced by using role-play. Instead of describing the problem the mother, Andrea, is invited to illustrate what happens in role-play. She is invited to play the role of her child, Joan, not going to bed and the facilitator, directed by Andrea, role-plays her original responses, not coping in the same manner. The exercise is then followed up with a group brainstorm of possible solutions, with Andrea selecting the response that provides the best 'fit' to her own situation. This is then practised in a solution role-play; but this time the roles are reversed: the parent is now in the role of the coping, successful parent and the facilitator is the compliant child!

Case Example 8.2 shows the benefits of using role-play and in particular how it can be used to move from a problem to a solution-focus. Some clients are immersed in their problem and cannot immediately switch to considering solutions. The above role-play sequence often has the positive effect of breaking this 'stuckness'. It generally introduces humour (clients think it is hilarious to see facilitators in role-play!) which in itself can free a problem focus. Secondly, in the guise of the other significant person (in the above example a child), the problem role-play allows the client to express their frustrated feelings, while at the same time beginning to empathise with the other person's perspective. Thirdly, by seeing the facilitator not providing an 'expert' answer, struggling in the same situation as themselves, the client's sense of isolation or being blamed can be reduced. Fourthly, this has a subtle reciprocal effect on the facilitator and the group audience, allowing them to understand better the parent's perspective. The general result is an increase in rapport, which frees up the client to consider the situation from a solution perspective, and thereby accept the suggestion to complete the solution role-play. The whole sequence reinforces clients' expertise, empowering them as the solvers of the problem.

Using role-play in skills practice
There are many other ways to introduce role-play into group process. In many psycho-educational groups a 'skills practice' section is structured into each group session, during which members are invited to practice in small groups or pairs the ideas covered in the session, particularly role-playing how they might carry them out at home. For example, during an assertiveness group, participants may practice in small groups how they are going to say a respectful 'no' to someone who intimidates them. By working in small groups, there is

ample opportunity for people to receive constructive feedback on their approach and sufficient time for everyone to participate.

Solution pictures/mind mapping

Visual images or symbols, which represent a solution or a particular strength, can be much more meaningful and evocative than words alone and thus can powerfully move clients to thinking differently and/or mobilise them to action. In this way using art or drawing exercises in groupwork can add depth and richness to solution generation. Many facilitators have designed creative and innovative ways of doing this. For example, mind mapping (Buzan & Buzan, 1993) is a creative thinking procedure that uses both words and images as a way of both recording information and generating new ideas and possibilities. Mind maps of solutions can be generated in the following way (see Figures 8.1 and 8.2):

1   A central image, and/or symbol or name, which represents the solution is selected and placed in the centre of the page.
2   The client free-associates around the solution, listing keywords and secondary images which represent the solution and its effects.
3   The keywords are linked to the central image by lines of varying thickness and colour, depending on the significance to the client.
4   Further keywords, associations, pictures, symbols can be added to enrich the detail of the map.

The power of mind maps lies in 1) how they combine both words and images thus appealing to different parts of the brain; 2) how they are radial and associative thus matching the natural thinking process; 3) how they can be compressed on small piece of paper; and 4) how they can be made unique and personally meaningful to different individuals.

Mind maps can be applied to groupwork in a number of ways. Sometimes generating a 'solution map' with clients can be sufficient to help them develop a better understanding of their goals and the next steps to achieve them. However, sometimes it is helpful to go through the preliminary step of creating a 'problem map' first. By creating a representation outside themselves, clients immersed in the problem narrative can achieve some helpful distance and perspective from which to consider action. (This is similar to the process of 'externalising the problem' as described in narrative therapy (White & Epston, 1990).) In addition, as illustrated below, a problem map can also generate 'clues' about the eventual solution.

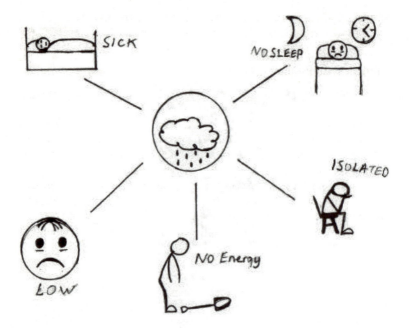

Figure 8.1   *Mind map of 'depression'*

Mind mapping in groupwork

1   The facilitator models the procedure of building a mind map, using a real example volunteered by one of the group members which is relevant to everyone else. The facilitator, using a flip chart, goes through the steps of building the mind map, adding the clients ideas and images as he/she goes along.

2   The clients are encouraged to build a mind map around the problem that they wish to solve. (See Figure 8.1 for an example on depression.)

3   The resultant mind maps are reviewed in the group and key points noted and shared.

4   Clients are now invited to build the 'solution map' which captures the goal they are seeking. If stuck they can consider the clues generated by the 'problem map'. For example, they can simply 'flip' the problem keywords and images and explore how the opposite descriptions might belong to the 'solution map' (see Figure 8.2).

5   The resultant mind maps are reviewed in the group and key points noted and shared.

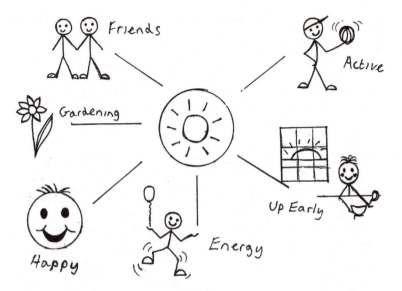

Figure 8.2   *Mind map of 'A good day'*

6   It can be helpful to finish with a final mind map on steps clients can take to get to the solution, or on examples of the solution already occurring in their lives.

Self-modelling using video

Making video recordings of group sessions for later review with clients is a long established technique in groupwork (Yalom, 1995). Generally whole sessions are recorded but the therapist selects key segments for review at a later group meeting. For example, a therapist may choose to review an assertiveness skills exercise, which included role-play, thus giving clients direct feedback on how they communicated and interacted.

In solution-focused groupwork the therapist is interested in selecting segments for review that provide constructive feedback, that is, segments which illustrate the client being successful or skilful or examples of group process where the group was supportive or cohesive. The video recording facilitates an 'exception' – which may have been unnoticed or forgotten – to receive extra attention and analysis. In essence, the video recording, which is paused and thoroughly reviewed, can 'slow down' group process to allow 'micro-solutions' to be understood and cultivated. For example, the video review of a client successfully completing an assertiveness exercise can last half an hour whereas the original exercise may have been only minutes long. Rather than relying on verbally expressed memory, video review can re-enact 'exceptions', allowing clients to witness the rich detail which they may not have remembered. It is truly strengths-based as clients are given an opportunity to learn from and model their own solutions. They literally become their own teacher.

Case Example 8.3   The Hanen Program

The Hanen Program (Manolson, 1992) is a psycho-educational group to empower parents to promote language development in their young children with language delays. It uses strengths-based teaching principles that have a resonance with the solution-focused approach. Central to the format is the use of videotape recordings. Parents are videotaped interacting with their children and this tape is reviewed individually with them and also within the group. However, the therapist primarily selects examples of supportive and effective communication between parent and child for review. For example, the therapist identifies examples on the videotape, even if they are brief, where the parent follows the child's lead, or makes a successful connection and these are explored in the review with questions such as:

● What is happening here?
● What did you do here that seemed to work?
● How did you go about doing this?
● What skill does this display?

In this way, the parents are invited to learn from their own examples of successful communication and from those of others in the group. Rather than exclusively learning from experts communicating with children, the parents are invited to self-model and to learn from their own expertise, thus building on their own strengths and confidence.

Summary

This chapter has outlined five creative exercises and activities which can be a useful addition to solution-focused groups in introducing novelty to a 'stuck' group process, in helping members work creatively together (and thus building group cohesion) and in mobilising the group's resources on creative solution building. The list is by no means exhaustive and facilitators are encouraged to creatively develop their own exercises that fit with the client group they work with. However, it is important to recognise that structured exercises themselves are not central to effective groups, but rather the *constructive group process* they can bring about. For this reason facilitators should not be dependent upon them or insist they are always done. Indeed, creative exercises can be unhelpful in groups if they do not fit with the group culture or members feel uncomfortable carrying them out. The ideal is to use exercises which emerge naturally from the group process, and which when timed correctly introduce just enough novelty to help group members move to the next stage in solution building.

References

American Counselling Association. (1995). *Code of ethics and standards of practice.* Alexandria, VA: American Counselling Association.

Assay, T.P., & Lambert, M.J. (1999). The empirical case for the common factors in therapy: Quantitative findings. In M.L. Hubble, B.L. Duncan, & S.D. Miller (Eds.), *The heart and soul of change: what works in therapy.* Washington, DC: American Psychological Association.

Bachelor, A. (1991). Comparison and relationship to outcome of diverse dimensions of the helping alliance as seen by client and therapist. *Psychotherapy, 28,* 534–49.

Badaines, A. (1988). Psychodrama. In J. Rowan and W. Dryden (Eds.), *Innovative therapy in Britain.* Milton Keynes: Open University.

Barber, J. (1977). Rapid induction analgesia: a clinical report. *American Journal of Clinical Hypnosis, 19* (3), 138–47.

Barker, P. (1992). *Basic family therapy* (3rd edn). Oxford: Blackwell.

Barkham, M.C., Evans, C., Margison, F., McGrath, G., Mellor-Clarke, J., Milne, D., & Connell, J. (1998). The rationale for developing and implementing core outcome batteries for routine use in service settings and psychotherapy outcome research. *Journal of Mental Health, 7,* 35–48.

Barkham, M., Shapiro, D.A., Hardy, G.E., & Rees, A. (1999). Psychotherapy in two-plus-one sessions: outcomes of a randomised controlled trial of cognitive-behavioral and psychodynamic-interpersonal therapy for subsyndromal depression. *Journal of Consulting and Clinical Psychology, 67* (2), 201–11.

Beck, A.T., Steer, R.A., & Garbin, M.G. (1988). Psychometric properties of the Beck Depression Inventory: twenty-five years of evaluation. *Clinical Psychology Review, 8,* 77–100.

Bednar, R.L., & Kaul, T.J. (1994). Experiential group research: can the canon catch fire? In A. Bergin, & S. Garfield (Eds.), *Handbook of psychotherapy and behavioral change.* New York: Wiley.

Berg, I.K. (1991). *Family preservation: a brief therapy workbook.* London: Brief Therapy Press.

Berg, I.K. (1994). *Family-based services: a solution-focused approach.* New York: W.W. Norton.

Berg, I.K. (1995). *I'd hear laughter.* (Video). New York: W.W. Norton.

Berg, I.K. (1999, 8–9 October). *Solution focused therapy.* University College Dublin, Ireland.

Berg, I.K., & Miller, S.D. (1992). *Working with the problem drinker: a solution focused approach.* New York: W.W. Norton.

Berne, E. (1966). *Principles of group treatment.* New York: Grove Press.

Bion, W. (1961). *Experience in groups and other papers.* London: Tavistock.

Brigitte, Sue, Mem & Veronika. (1997). Power to our journeys. *Dulwich Centre Newsletter,* 345 Carrington Street, Adelaide, South Australia 5000, 1, 25–34.

Budman, S.H., & Gurman, A.S. (1988). *Theory and practice of brief psychotherapy.* New York: Guilford Press.

Buzan, T., & Buzan, B. (1993). *The mind map book.* London: BBC.

Campbell, T.C., & Brasher, B. (1994). The pause that refreshes: opportunities, interventions and predictions in group therapy with cocaine addicts. *Journal of Systemic Therapies, 13* (2), 65–73.

Colgan McCarthy, I., & O'Reilly Byrne, N. (1995). A spell in the fifth province. In S. Friedman (Ed.), *Reflecting team in action.* New York: Guilford.

Conyne, R.K. (1999). *Failures in groupwork: how we can learn from our mistakes.* California: Sage.

Core System Group. (1998). *CORE System (Information Management) Handbook.* Leeds: Core System Group.

Corey, G. (2000). *Theory and practice of group counselling* (5th edn). Pacific Grove, CA: Brooks/Cole Wadsworth.

de Shazer, S. (1984). The death of resistance. *Family Process, 23,* 30–40.

de Shazer, S. (1985). *Keys to solution in brief therapy* (1st edn). New York: W.W. Norton.

de Shazer, S. (1988). *Clues: investigating solutions in brief therapy* (1st edn). New York: W.W. Norton.

de Shazer, S. (1994). *Words were originally magic* (1st edn). New York: W.W. Norton.

de Shazer, S., & Berg, I.K. (1997). 'What works': remarks on research aspects of solution-focused brief therapy. *Journal of Family Therapy, 19* (2), 121–4.

de Shazer, S., Berg, I.F., Lipchik, E., Nunnally, F., Molnar, A., Gingerich, W.J., & Weiner-Davis, M. (1986). Brief therapy: focused solution development. *Family Process, 25,* 207–21.

Dolan, Y.M. (1991). *Resolving sexual abuse: solution focused therapy and Ericksonian hypnosis for adult survivors* (1st edn). New York: Norton.

Duncan, B.L., Hubble, M.A., & Miller, S.D. (1997). *Psychotherapy with 'impossible' cases: the efficient treatment of therapy veterans* (1st edn). New York: Norton.

Duncan, B.L., & Miller, S.D. (2000). *The heroic client: doing client-directed, outcome-informed therapy.* San Francisco: Jossey-Bass.

Forehand, R.L., & McMahon, R.J. (1981). *Helping the noncompliant child: a clinician's guide to parent training.* New York: Guilford.

Freeman, J., & Combs, G. (1996). *Narrative therapy: the social construction of preferred realities.* New York: Norton.

Freeman, J., Epston, D., & Lobovits, D. (1997). *Playful approaches to serious problems: narrative therapy with children and families.* New York: Norton.

Froyd, J.E., & Lambert, M.J. (1989). *A survey of outcome research measures in psychotherapy research.* Paper presented at the Western Psychological Association, Reno, NV.

Furman, B., & Ahola, T. (1992). *Solution talk: hosting therapeutic conversations.* New York: Norton.

Furman, B., & Ahola, T. (1997). *Succeeding together: solution-oriented team building.* Helsinki: International Reteaming Institute.

Garfield, S., & Bergin, A. (1994). *Handbook of psychotherapy and behavioral change* (4th edn). New York: Wiley.

Gawain, S. (1995). *Creative visualization.* San Rafael, California: New World Library.

Gazda, G.M. (1989). *Group counseling: a developmental approach* (4th edn). Boston: Allyn & Bacon.

George, E. (24–28 February 1998). Solution-focused therapy training seminar. Maynooth, Ireland.

George, E., Iveson, C., & Ratner, H. (1990). *Problem to solution: brief therapy with individuals and families.* London: Brief Therapy Press.

Gergen, K.J., & McNamee, S. (Eds.). (1992). *Therapy as social construction.* London: Sage.

Gladding, S.T. (1991). *Group work: a counseling speciality.* New York: Macmillan.

Goodman, G., & Jacobs, M. (1994). The self-help, mutual support group. In A. Fuhriman & G.M. Burlingame (Eds.), *Handbook of group psychotherapy.* New York: Wiley.

Goodman, R. (1997). The strengths and difficulties questionnaire: a research note. *Journal of Child Psychology and Psychiatry, 38* (4).

Greenberg, R.P., & Fisher, S. (1997). Mood-mending medicines: probing drug, psychotherapy and placebo solutions. In R.P. Greenberg, & S. Fisher (Eds.), *From placebo to panacea: putting psychiatric drugs to the test.* New York: Wiley.

Grieves, L. (1998). From beginning to start: the Vancouver anti-anorexia/anti-bulimia league. In S. Madigan, & I. Law (Eds.), *Praxis: situating discourse, feminism & politics in narrative therapies.* Vancouver: Yaletown Family Therapy.

Gurman, A.S. (1977). The patient's perception of the therapeutic relationship. In A.S. Gurman, & A.M. Razin (Eds.), *Effective psychotherapy.* New York: Pergamon.

Houston, G. (1984). *The red book of groups.* London: Rochester Foundation.

Hovarth, A.O., & Greenberg, L.S. (1989). Development and validation of the working alliance inventory. *Journal of Counselling Psychology, 36,* 223–33.

Hoyt, M.F. (1995). *Brief therapy and managed care: readings for contemporary practice* (1st edn). San Francisco: Jossey-Bass.

Hurley, J. (1989). Affiliativeness and outcome in interpersonal groups: member and leader perspectives. *Psychotherapy, 26,* 520–23.

Isabeart, L., & de Shazer, S. (1997). (unpublished paper). A solution focused approach to the treatment of alcohol problems: The Bruges model.

Iveson, C. (1998). *Solution-focused supervision.* Paper presented at the European Brief Therapy Association Conference, Salamanca, Spain.

Jenkins, A. (1990). *Invitations to responsibility: the therapeutic engagement of men who are violent and abusive.* Adelaide: Dulwich Centre Publications.

Johnson, D.W., & Johnson, F.P. (1994). *Joining together: group theory and group skills.* Boston: Allyn & Bacon.

Johnson, L.D. (1994). *Session Rating Scale.* Salt Lake City: Author.

Klein, R. (1993). Short-term group psychotherapy. In H. Kaplan, & D. Sadock (Eds.), *Comprehensive group psychotherapy.* Baltimore: Williams and Wilkins.

Koss, M.P., & Shiang, J. (1994). Research on brief psychotherapy. In S. Garfield, & A. Bergin (Eds.), *Handbook of psychotherapy and behavioral change.* New York: Wiley.

Koumans, A.J.R., Muller, J.J., & Miller, C.F. (1967). Use of telephone calls to increase motivation for treatment in alcoholics. *Psychological Reports, 21,* 327–28.

Kral, R. (1988). Solution identification scale. Milwaukee, Wisconsin: Brief Family Therapy Centre.

Krupnick, J.L., Sotsky, S.M., Simmens, S., Moyher, J., Elkin, I., Watkins, J., & Pilkonis, P.A. (1996). The role of the therapeutic alliance in psychotherapy and pharmacotherapy outcome: findings in the National Institute of Mental Health Treatment of Depression Collaborative Research Project. *Journal of Consulting and Clinical Psychology, 64,* 532–9.

LaFontain, R. (1999). Solution focused therapy. In J. Donigan, & D. Hulse-Killacky (Eds.), *Critical incidents in group therapy*. Belmont, CA: Wadsworth.

LaFontain, R., & Garner, N. (1996). Solution-focused counseling groups: the results are in. *Journal for Specialists in Group Work, 21*, 128–43.

LaFontain, R., Garner, N., & Boldosser, S. (1995). Solution-focused counseling groups for children and adolescents. *Journal of Systemic Therapies, 14* (4), 39–51.

LaFontain, R., Garner, N., & Eliason, G. (1996). Solution-focused counseling groups: a key for school counsellors. *The School Counsellor, 42*, 256–67.

Lambert, M., Burlingame, G., Umphress, V., Vermeersch, D., Clouse, G., & Yanchar, S. (1996). The reliability and validity of the Outcome Questionnaire. *Clinical Psychology and Psychotherapy, 3* (4), 249–58.

Lambert, M.J. (1992). Implications of outcome research for psychotherapy integration. In J.C. Norcross, & M.R. Goldfried (Eds.), *Handbook of psychotherapy integration*. New York: Basic Books.

Lawson, D. (1994). Identifying pre-treatment change. *Journal of Counselling and Development, 72*, 244–8.

Lee, M., Greene, G.J., Uken, A., Sebold, J., & Rheinscheld, J. (1997). *Solution-focused brief group treatment of domestic violence offenders*. Paper presented at the Four-in-One Conference, Bruge, Belgium.

Lewin, K. (1951). *Field theory in social science*. New York: Harper.

Lieberman, M.A., Yalom, I.D., & Miles, M.B. (1973). *Encounter groups: first facts*. New York: Basic Books.

Lipchik, E. (1994). The rush to be brief. *Networker* (March/April), pp. 35–9.

Lundgren, D., & Miller, D. (1965). Identity and behavioral changes in training groups. *Human Relations Training News* (Spring).

MacKenzie, K.R. (Ed.). (1994). *Effective use of group psychotherapy in managed care*. Washington DC: American Psychiatric Press.

Madigan, S. (1998). *A narrative approach to anorexia* (1st edn). San Francisco, CA: Jossey-Bass.

Malamud, D., & Machover, S. (1965). *Toward self-understanding*. Springfield, IL: Charles C. Thomas.

Manolson, A. (1992). *It takes two to talk: the Hanen program for parents of children with language delays*. Toronto: The Hanen Centre, Suite 403–1075 Bay Street, Toronto, ON M5S 2B1, Canada, www.hanen.org.

McCallum, M., Piper, W., & Joyce, A. (1992). Dropping out from short-term group therapy. *Psychotherapy, 29*, 206–13.

McRoberts, C., Burlingame, G.M., & Hoag, M.J. (1998). Comparative efficacy of individual and group psychotherapy: a meta-analytic perspective. *Group Dynamics, 2* (2), 101–17.

Meissen, G.J., Mason, W.C., & Gleason, D.F. (1991). Understanding the attitudes and intentions of future professionals toward self-help. *American Journal of Community Psychology, 19* (5), 699–714.

Metcalf, L. (1998). *Solution focused group therapy: ideas for groups in private practice, schools, agencies and treatment programs*. New York: Free Press.

Miller, S.D. (1998). *Psychotherapy with impossible cases*. Paper presented at the Brief Therapy Conference, Dublin.

Miller, S.D., Duncan, B.L., & Hubble, M.A. (1997). *Escape from Babel: toward a unifying language for psychotherapy practice*. New York: Norton.

Miller, W.R., & Rollnick, S. (1991). *Motivational interviewing: preparing people to change addictive behavior*. New York: Guilford.

Moreno, J.L. (1964). *Psychodrama: Volume 1* (2nd edn). New York: Beacon.

Nirenberg, T.D., Sobell, L.C., & Sobell, M.B. (1980). Effective and inexpensive procedures for decreasing client attrition in outpatient alcohol treatment program. *American Journal of Drug and Alcohol Abuse, 7*, 73–82.

Nylund, D., & Corsiglia, V. (1994). Becoming solution-forced in brief therapy: remembering something important we already knew. *Journal of Systemic Therapies, 13* (1), 5–12.

O'Connell, B. (1998). *Solution-focused therapy*. London: Sage.

O'Hanlon, W.H., & Weiner-Davies, M. (1989). *In search of solutions: a new direction in psychotherapy*. New York: Norton.

Orlinsky, D.E., Grawe, K., & Park, B.K. (1994). Process and outcome in psychotherapy – noch enimal. In A.E. Bergin, & S.L. Garfield (Eds.), *Handbook of psychotherapy and behavioral change* (4th edn). New York: Wiley.

Patterson, G.R., & Forgatch, M.S. (1985). Therapist behaviour as a determinant for client non-compliance: a paradox for the behavior modifier. *Journal of Consulting and Clinical Psychology, 53*, 846–51.

Perls, F. (1967). Group vs. individual therapy. *A Review of General Semantics, 24*, 306–12.

Perry, J. (1992). Problems and considerations in the valid assessment of personality disorders. *American Journal of Psychiatry, 149*, 1645–53.

Piper, W. (1994). Client Variables. In A. Fuhrman, & G. Burlingame (Eds.), *Handbook of group psychotherapy*. New York: Wiley.

Prochaska, J.O., & DiClemente, C.C. (1992). The transtheoretical approach. In J.C. Norcross, & M.R. Goldfried (Ed.), *Handbook of psychotherapy integration*. New York: Basic Books.

Prochaska, J.O., DiClemente, C.C., & Norcross, J.C. (1992). In search of how people change: applications to addictive behaviors. *American Psychologist, 47* (9), 1102–14.

Quinn, M., & Quinn, T. (1995). *The nought to sixes parenting programme*. Newry: Family Caring Trust.

Rappaport, J., Reischl, T.M., & Zimmerman, M.A. (1992). Mutual help mechanisms in the empowerment of former mental patients. In D. Saleeby (Ed.), *The strengths perspective in social work*. New York: Longman.

Rogers, C. (1970). *Carl Rogers on encounter groups*. New York: Harper & Row.

Rogers, C.R. (1986). Client-centred therapy. In I.L. Kutash, & A. Wolf (Eds.), *Psychotherapist's casebook*. San Francisco: Jossey-Bass.

Rose, S.D. (1998). *Group therapy with troubled youth: a cognitive-behavioral interactive approach*. California: Sage.

Rosenberg, S., & Zimet, C. (1995). Brief group treatment and managed mental health care. *International Journal of Group Psychotherapy, 45*, 367–79.

Rossi, E. (1980). *Collected papers of Milton Erickson on hypnosis* (Volume 4). New York: Irvington.

Saleeby, D. (Ed.). (1992). *The strengths perspective in social work*. New York: Longman.

Saleeby, D. (1996). The strengths perspective in social work practice: extensions and cautions. *Social Work, 41* (3), 296–305.

Sangharakshita. (1996). *The Buddha's victory*. Birmingham: Windhorse Publications.

Schoor, M. (1995). Finding solutions in a relaxation group. *Journal of Systemic Therapies, 14* (4), 55–63.

Schoor, M. (1997). Finding solutions in a roomful of angry people. *Journal of Systemic Therapies*, *16* (3), 201–10.

Schubert, M.A., & Borkman, T.J. (1991). An organisational typology for self-help groups. *American Journal of Community Psychology*, *19* (5), 769–87.

Scott, M.J., & Stradling, S.G. (1998). *Brief group counselling: integrating individual and group cognitive-behavioural approaches*. Chichester: Wiley.

Selekman, M. (1993). *Pathways to change: brief therapy solutions with difficult adolescents*. New York: Guilford.

Selekman, M.D. (1997). *Solution-focused therapy with children: Harnessing family strengths for systemic change*. New York: Guilford.

Sharry, J. (1999). Towards solution groupwork. *Journal of Systemic Therapies*, *18* (2), 77–91.

Sharry, J. (in press). Solution-focused parent training. In O'Connell, B. (Ed.), *Solution focused therapy in practice*. London: Sage.

Sharry, J., Madden, B., Darmody, M., Miller, S.D., & Duncan, B. (in press). Giving our clients the break: applications of client-directed outcome-informed clinical work. *Journal of Systemic Therapies*.

Shepard, M. (1992). Predicting batterer recidivism five years after community intervention. *Journal of Family Violence*, *7*, 167–78.

Smith, M.L., Glass, G.V., & Miller, T.I. (1980). *The Benefits of Psychotherapy*. Baltimore: Johns Hopkins University.

Snyder, C.R., Michael, S.T., & Cleavins, J.S. (1999). Hope as a psychotherapeutic foundation of common factors, placebos and expectancies. In M.L. Hubble, B.L. Duncan, & S.D. Miller (Eds.), *The heart and soul of change: what works in therapy*. Washington, DC: American Psychological Association.

Stockton, R., & Toth, P.L. (1999). The case for group research. In J.P. Trotzer (Ed.), *The counsellor and the group: integrating theory, training and practice* (3rd edn). Philadelphia: Taylor and Francis.

Stone, W., & Rutan, S. (1983). Duration of treatment in group psychotherapy. *International Journal of Group Psychotherapy*, *34*, 109.

Toseland, R., & Siporin, M. (1986). When to recommend group treatment. *International Journal of Group Psychotherapy*, *36*, 171–201.

Tuckman, B.W. (1965). Developmental sequence in small groups. *Psychological Bulletin*, *63*, 384–99.

Tudor, K. (1999). *Group Counselling*. London: Sage.

Uken, A. (1999). Recidivism rates at seven year follow-up. Personal Communication, 7th October 1999.

Uken, A., & Sebold, J. (1996). The Plumas Project: a solution focused goal-directed domestic violence diversion program. *Journal of Collaborative Therapies*, *4*, 10–17.

Van Bilsen, H.P.J.G. (1991). Motivational interviewing: perspectives from the Netherlands, with particular emphasis on heroin-dependent clients. In W.R. Miller, & S. Rollnick (Eds.), *Motivational Interviewing: preparing people to change addictive behaviour*. New York: Guilford.

Vaughn, K., Hastings-Guerrero, S., & Kassner, C. (1996). Solution-oriented inpatient group therapy. *Journal of Systemic Therapies*, *15* (3), 1–14.

Wade, A. (1997). Small acts of living: everyday resistance to violence and other forms of oppression. *Contemporary Family Therapy*, *19* (1).

Walsh, F. (1996). The concept of family resilience: crisis and challenge. *Family Process*, *35* (3), 261–81.

Walsh, T. (Ed.). (1997). *Solution focused child protection – towards a positive frame for social work practice*. Dublin: Department of Social Studies, University of Dublin, Trinity College.

Walter, J.L., & Peller, J.E. (1992) *Becoming solution-focused in brief therapy*. New York: Brumer/Mazel.

Watzlawick, P., Weakland, J., & Fisch, R. (1974). *Change: principles of problem formation and problem resolution*. New York: Norton.

Webster-Stratton, C., & Herbert, M. (1994). *Troubled Families Problem Children*. Chichester: Wiley.

Weiner-Davies, M., de Shazer, S., & Gingerich, W.J. (1987). Using pre-treatment change to construct a therapeutic solution: a clinical note. *Journal of Marital and Family Therapy*, *13* (4), 359–63.

White, M., & Epston, D. (1990). *Narrative means to therapeutic ends*. New York: Norton.

Wuthnow, R. (1994). *Sharing the Journey*. New York: Free Press.

Yalom, I.D. (1970). *The theory and practice of group psychotherapy*. New York: Basic Books.

Yalom, I.D. (1995). *The theory and practice of group psychotherapy* (4th edn). New York: Basic Books.

Yalom, I.D. (1999). *Momma and the meaning of life*. London: Piatkus.

Yalom, I.D., Houts, S., Zimerberg, S., & Rand, K. (1967). Prediction of improvement in group therapy. *Archives of General Psychiatry*, *17*, 159–68.

Zimmerman, T.S., Jacobsen, R.B., MacIntyre, M., & Watson, C. (1996). Solution-focused parenting groups: an empirical study. *Journal of Systemic Therapies*, *15*, 12–25.

Index